MW01283585

THE

Alabaster Jar

Denise Anderson

ISBN 978-1-64299-806-1 (paperback)
ISBN 978-1-64299-856-6 (hardcover)
ISBN 978-1-64299-807-8 (digital)

Copyright © 2018 by Denise Anderson

All rights reserved. No part of this publication may be reproduced, distributed, or transmitted in any form or by any means, including photocopying, recording, or other electronic or mechanical methods without the prior written permission of the publisher. For permission requests, solicit the publisher via the address below.

Christian Faith Publishing, Inc.
832 Park Avenue
Meadville, PA 16335
www.christianfaithpublishing.com

Printed in the United States of America

To my children, *David, Jeff, and Susie*
who are the joy of my life

To my *magnificent seven grandchildren,*
who are the light of my life. Rule no. 4 forever.

To *Reverend Kenneth R. Kaucheck,*
spiritual father and sacred companion
guiding the way to living in Christ.

—AMDG

CONTENTS

III. Grace

IV. Prayer

V. Silence and Solitude

VI. Mystery

VII. Trust

VIII. Love

IX. Scripture

X. Abuse and Spirituality

XI. Advent and Christmas

XII. Easter

FOREWORD
BY REV. KENNETH KAUCHECK

Chapter 1 verse 29 in the gospel of John reads, "John the Baptist saw Jesus coming toward him and said, "Behold, the Lamb of God, who takes away the sins of the world." When John sees Jesus, it is not merely a physical sighting. He sees into the mission of Jesus. His seeing is a revelation, and so it begins with the word that triggers revelation, "Behold."

The book of poems that you now hold in your hand began with an experience the author had with that one word, "Behold." Revelation is like that. It begins with a word out of an experience and that word leads to another word which leads to more words which create the melodic flow of the poems which gives the reader an insight into the dynamic of the revelation.

In chapter 1 vv. 31-33 of the same gospel John the Baptist participated in Jesus' post-baptismal experience. He saw the Spirit come down like a dove from heaven and remain upon him. The description of the Spirit remaining upon Jesus signals that this is more than a momentary experience or a divine gift for a special task. The Spirit and Jesus are permanently connected. There is an important implication to this 'remaining' together of Jesus and the Spirit. So it is with this book of poems, "*The Alabaster Jar*."

The author of these poems, like all of us, would claim, like John the Baptist in chapter 1 of the gospel of John, that she did not know him. Although, like John the Baptist, she had an experience she could not interpret correctly. In other words, she did not know all that it meant. As in these poems this confusion is resolved by listening to the voice of God. As John heard the voice, so the author of these poems heard the voice. It is this voice that has spoken to the author of these poems and addresses the full meaning of the experience. It is God's voice that ultimately prompted the writing of these poems, a testimony that bears witness to the truth of the power of the Spirit in all of us. It is not a voice from heaven, but a voice through Denise Anderson. Human witnessing has replaced divine revelation.

The voice that creates the poems helps her to interpret what it is that she hears and sees. The gift of the experience. This means for us as we read these poems and bask in their power that Jesus is the giver of the Spirit. That through the Father the Spirit is given in Jesus who calls us to witness to the power of the experience we have in prayer. It is through Jesus that the divine Spirit enters the world and brings life. It is Jesus who sends us that Spirit and these poems, which now becomes our prayer and are a mirror reflection of the giving and receiving of that Spirit. Jesus sends the Spirit and that means that Jesus is the Son of God.

The divine voice aids our understanding and makes us ready to join all who speak of what we know and testify to what we have seen. However, our testimony and that of the author is situated within a double, interpersonal context. Each one of us will both witness to the truth that each of these poems speak to us and at the same time share what we have experienced from these poems to whomever will listen.

What is the purpose of these poems? I would propose for you that the purpose of this poetry, as is always true with God, is to attract others to God though Jesus. The words of the poems are the words of God. God is speaking to us through these words. God will take our desire and turn it into a calling. His invitation to us, "Come and see," is an invitation into a personal relationship of who He is. When we "stay" with Him we come into his revelation and receive it into the depths of our being.

I invite you now to begin this journey through this poetry and discover for yourself the truth about God, the truth about you, and let God now show you the way, "Behold."

(Rev.) Kenneth Kaucheck, J.C.D.D.min
January 23, 2018

INTRODUCTION

In order to better understand the depth and personal references in The Alabaster Jar, it's important to know some of my life story. Like every life, it has its deep blessings and graces. My three children, David, Jeff and Susie, are my greatest gifts. They have also blessed me with seven grandchildren who are the light of my life.

Also, like any life, it has had its dark nights and struggles with faith: divorce, sexual abuse, PTSD (thank you, John Bernardo). The death of David, my first born who died in a car accident at age nineteen, was the most difficult of all. He is a gift of love and grace.

We are blessed to have a Jesuit retreat house, Manresa, in the local area. After becoming a spiritual director, I trained to give the spiritual exercises of St. Ignatius, which I continue to do today. It is a great grace to be a companion to people on their journey. For fifteen years, I studied Christian Spiritual Classics with Reverend Bernie Owens, SJ, author of <u>More Than You Can Ever Imagine</u> On Our Becoming Divine (Liturgical Press).

The writings are prayers, insights, enlightenment, hope, and encouragement during the consolations and desolations of the spiritual journey.

Denise Anderson, 7/31

THE ALABASTER JAR

The woman with the alabaster jar
filled with her riches,
broke the jar and poured those
riches onto the feet of Jesus.

She poured herself out for the love
of her Savior.
She risked all her vulnerability
to enter the house and perform the anointing.

The poems in this book are the riches
the Holy Spirit fed to me.
I too risk vulnerability in breaking
them open to the public.

The relationship between the woman and Jesus
is a very blessed and sacred relationship.
My desire has always been one with hers.
I too wish to pour myself out for Christ.

This is my way of doing what she did.
What I love about the story is how Jesus accepted her.
He respected and received her love.
I pray that He receives my love as well.

—Denise Anderson

CHAPTER I

Longing For God

Gift of Desire

He wakes desire you may never forget;
He shows you stars you never saw before.
—Tennyson

How can the desire to return love for love,
that sears so deep into untouched corners
and channels of the heart be ever forgotten?

When the Spirit implants the longing to
be for God, love for God, work for God
it can be a dangerous thing.

Desire without commitment, without action
can turn into a pleasure all its own,
going nowhere except focusing on its self.

Desire with action and no commitment
going seemingly everywhere.
but nowhere except back into its self
seeking the relief from the burning within,
seems as fruitless as wind chimes without any wind.

Desire is like the first cry the baby screams for food.
The first smile for love.
The first step for movement.
It is only the beginning.

Do I dare trust it?
Believing it to be a gift embedded by the Spirit
giving me the strength to look out and up?
something I am utterly powerless to do on my own.

To see stars that I never knew were there.
People I never knew needed care.
Children who ache inside for a touch;
a smile, someone to even notice they exist.
The "incorrigible" child whom no one likes,
but somehow I always do.

Stars I never knew were there.
Love I never have risked before.
Commitments I have not dared to make.

Courage, now blessed by the Lord,
changes my life one act at a time,
one ordinary day at a time.
One blessing for all time.

God Heals Broken Hearts

God is a great healer of hearts that are broken.
I know for he has healed mine when needed.
There is only one catch,
your heart is left longing for Him.

Hungering for God is a pervasive reality.
It's more than a feeling.
It's an act of will.
It's an act of intellect.

When my heart has been healed by God,
I knew exactly who was doing the healing.
There was no mystery,
no wondering who it was.

The longing for God is on my mind,
in my heart,
and in my deepest desires.
I search for Him with all my being.

Nothing less than God can leave me satisfied.
Hunger for food leaves a gnawing pain inside.
Food is needed to fill that hunger.
hunger for God leaves a gnawing "wound" inside.

When the longing for God is at the center of my life,
it feeds my actions, thoughts, and feelings.
Things that used to satisfy
no longer do.

So I wait
and pray and beseech Him.
I know He will come again,
I just don't know when.

Until then, hunger for Him
consumes me.

Inner Flame

There are things that "happen" when sleep is coming.
Just now, I noticed that there was a flame
burning in my heart.
It appeared soon after the yearning started.

"It feels like…" the flame represents the longing.
The longing is the trigger that ignites the flame
and keeps it burning.
Could it be that it is a symbol of our love?

It is a slight flame that flickers inside.
It's more correct to say it is a gentle flame
that casts off a soft light.
It points straight upwards.

JFK has his "eternal flame."
This too is an eternal flame
whose purpose is to keep the love burning
well into eternity.

Loneliness or Longing?

At first I've been naming it loneliness,
I was thinking in the secular.
But I live in the Kingdom
so things are a little different.

Thinking of all the things that could
fill the loneliness made me realize
there is only One
who can fill such a hole.

Realizing it was only Christ who could ease this ache,
I realized it was a yearning for him,
not a loneliness the world can fill.

It's hard to go back and forth between the worlds,
but being "the beloved child of God,"
is very different from just being a person retired.
The paradigm turns upside down.

All the experiences, revelations, unions are
not in the past. There is no time with God.
They may have happened in my past,
but God only deals with the past being me in the present.

How do I dare forget that?
It belittles His gifts, and I become ungrateful
For the very greatest of all gifts—
Oneness in Him.

I long to be the contemplative that lives in no time,
and accepts that God's ways are not my ways.
the daughter, the spouse, who always turns to God
with her hands open, receiving whatever He deems best.

"My Lord and My God"

This is not the first time
I have written about these words.
It is the phrase that is
my most frequent prayer.

As they started again tonight,
I thought to reflect on why I was praying them.
There were no other words.
I wanted no other words.

The longing is there,
the desire to just "be with"
in a stillness free of any other words,
any other ideas.

When the desire for prayer
reaches such simplicity,
"My Lord and my God"
says it all with the least amount of words.

There is a hunger for there to be
few, if any, words and ideas.
It is Jesus pulling me into silent contemplation,
free of *all* words, thoughts, and ideas.

Maybe they come when I don't sense His Presence,
but want nothing more than to pray.
I really don't know why,
but I do know it does not matter.

No Place to Stay

"Where do you stay?" they asked Jesus.
"Come and follow me" was his reply.
They found out that He stayed nowhere.
He was always on the move,
teaching, preaching, and healing.
"The Son of Man has nowhere to lay his head."

"Come and follow me," he invites over and over.
I too want to know where he stays, so I follow.
and like the others, follow and keep following, for he does not stop
and does not expect us to stop once we say "Yes."

Why?
Why do I keep going when it gets tiring and every old insecurity
within me screams, "This isn't a place at all that we are going!"

When I get the nerve to face my fears to answer that question,
the answer comes from within and beyond me.
You are right. There is no place,
there is no place to stay

But I need and long to stay with him,
so keep going despite the doubts, the taunts,
the fact it makes no sense.

Or does it make sense?
It makes all the sense in the world when I am with him,
for I love him.
and in the loving him find out he is going "somewhere."
and he truly does have a place to stay.

He showed us by how he lived his life.
He was going to the Father and in his going
it is in the Father he stayed.
This is the same place he calls us to follow
and he now stays with us as we stumble to do what he did.

Sometimes I get scared, nervous, tired…
but the Epiphany homily allows me to keep going:
"He never asks us to go anywhere where he will not be with us."
There truly is a covenant—built on trust and love.
The "place" of the covenant is in him.

Restless Souls

Restless souls behind hearts that are broken,
reaching out to be soothed and calmed.

Restless souls that need a sheltering home
to hearts long ago abandoned and left to weep alone.

A soul both restless and still
finds its stillness, prepares, and awaits
a tabernacle of presence for her God.

Yet the very Presence is what arouses
the restlessness of her longing.

Images and feelings pass in and through her heart,
but must leave their imprint at the doorstep,
for the soul tolerates no metaphors, no images
they fall short and drift away.

The soul is stillness and silence
awaiting the Presence that is pure.
Union so precious
it can only be shared in silence.

It makes no sense
yet it is the very Presence that arouses
even greater the restlessness of her longing.

Thirst for God

Dry, parched, fatigue…
why keep going?
But how could I not after being
cradled in His tenderness?
Sensing the fullness of Oneness.

When led into the desert,
why keep wandering its barrenness?
Yet it feels the very roaming in such starkness
intensifies the need to find the Root of all Life.

Parched thirst is quenched
by stored up tears.
He promised Living Water.

Poverty of life in dry land
teaches to find and cherish all life.
The loneliness of the journey
lifts my vision from my own narrow pain
into the pain of others.
The joy and love of others
the sacredness of all others.

He who is the Root of all Life,
Is present in all life.
This is where He abides.
It is there we are found.

We Already Have It Inside

"All that we need is inside"
our pastor used to preach in his homilies.
Turning our search for God from outside to inside.

It seems such a paradox,
yet nothing makes more sense.
How could we be hungry and searching for Someone
unless we had already experienced Him?

We wouldn't recognize Him
when He made sure we discovered Him
living silently and majestically
within our inner tabernacles.

A very poor analogy is the game of "hide and seek."
We go looking for the person we already know.
We hope to find him or her before time runs out.
Happily God lives in a world outside of time.

How desperately we all search,
we begin our searching sometimes
without even knowing what we are searching for.
We are all "hardwired" to seek our Creator.

Imagine if you will, the reaction
of the prodigal son when he saw his father on the lookout for him.
"Commonly first we fall and later we see it
and both are the mercy of God." (J. of Norwich)

The mercy of God inspires and drives our search.
It is the mercy and love of God
that opens us up to be received
into the tenderness of His welcoming love.

—

What Are You Looking For?

Can the answer be as simple as
"I am looking for You"?
You are much talked about in the towns and villages.
Your followers are different in some way.

I want to be like them, like You.
Committed, passionate, driven yet in peace.
This is such a unique combination
and I want to be a part of Your Way.

I have been following at a distance,
but paying great attention to Your Group.
Sometimes people ask to join you,
and the answer is "No."

I want to join you more than anything
I have ever wanted before…
but I fear
you might say no and then I will be lost.

When is the right time to approach you?
I ask some of the women,
they smile welcoming smiles but shrug their shoulders.
Then one day I see your Mother in the crowd.

Surely she will be able to tell me what to do.
She listens to me carefully and gives a nod of assurance.
She said that her Son will see the purity
of the longing in my heart and I should not worry.

As you do quite often, I see you draw apart to pray.
Not daring to interrupt you in prayer,
I wait until you are walking back to the group,
and approach you.

"What do you seek?"
"I seek only You, Lord."
"And nothing else?" He asks.
"No, just You for then I would have everything."

—

What Do You Seek?

Is the title of the book by my bedside.
It has been there for a few weeks
and I guess the title has been playing in my unconscious.
What do you seek?

My mind came up with ideas,
but I quickly dismissed them.
They did not seem important enough.
The only answer I can think of is "You."

I seek You, Lord,
for all else compared to you is senseless.
Don't get me wrong,
I love my family, friends, and home.

Yet any of those without Christ carries
no meaning in of themselves.
It is because of loving them in Him
that gives them their deeper meaning.

I don't mean to play word games or write riddles.
Perhaps it is more correct to say
that because of Christ I know how to love
and therefore love much deeper.

Although Christ had "nowhere to lay his head,"
he did not ask everyone to follow him in that lifestyle.
My vocation has been to be a single mother,
now a grandmother to seven.

Loving others makes us vulnerable.
To tell the Lord I seek Him
makes us both vulnerable.
The romantic side of love is glorified in books and shows.

The real risk in loving is its vulnerability.
That is the true beauty of love.
We give all of ourselves
or it isn't real Love.

—

My Prayer Book

These writings cannot just be sent off in the mail
or added to a notebook.
That is not the reason they are given to me.
Once written, they must be pondered and prayed.

The writing is the quick and easy part.
The Spirit gives them to me for a deeper reason.
They are given to me as lessons,
lessons that must be integrated into living.

My notebook is not a collection of papers,
but a prayer book to be pondered.
It means taking the time to go back
and ponder the words that were given.

—

CHAPTER II

Holy Spirit

"Be Still and Know That I Am God"

It's silly for me to search for words
when they have already been placed in Scripture
and say exactly what the inner movement
is doing.

Yesterday, at the hairdresser, I could feel God stir.
At first I panicked because of not having the computer
but that was good because all He wanted was for me to
"Be still and know that I am God."

There is much more stirring within
than there has been before.
Perhaps it is better to say that I notice the Spirit moving.
It is sacred adoration taking place within.

His only request is that I notice, pay attention,
and then let it be.
There is no pattern to the Spirit's
comings and goings.

I suspect that the Spirit has made me more sensitive
to the inner movements.
In the middle of the hairdresser with all the noise?
In the middle of shopping at the mall?

Yesterday I noticed that by paying attention to the inner movement,
it would connect me to some of the outer happenings.
The care of the hairdresser and his assistant,
the warmth made me think of the warmth of God.

It feels like living gently in the Trinity.
Different from being pulled into the creative power of force.
The world takes on a different face and pace.
All is gentle and soft.

Beyond Pentecost

The first realization for the disciples
was probably the move from fear to resolve.
They went from hiding for their safety
to determination to preach the Word of their Lord.

Jesus told them of the Spirit to come
as well as the necessity for the Spirit to inspire their lives.
I would love to know what they thought
"the Spirit" meant.

That was the historical first Pentecost.
The number of Pentecosts since then are probably countless.
As with the disciples,
the Spirit comes to each one of us.

I recognize the Spirit in the strength and courage.
I know the Spirit has come when I humbly acknowledge
I am not in control of my life and its changes within.
There is someone else guiding me, and it is the Spirit.

Sometimes it is the movement from fear to confidence.
Other times when I am given the words in directing others.
Reading Acts, it appears the Presence was rather continuous.
I am finding it more constant in my own life.

Perhaps with the Wisdom that comes with age helps.
There is a knowing it is best to turn over life.
God is the reason why we live and for whom we live.
It's best to make the surrender continuous as we grow.

Tomorrow the church officially celebrates Pentecost.
Yet for those who pay attention,
it is celebrated every day of the year.
Thank you, Lord.

Living Litany

The idea that my life is a litany of gratitude
has really struck a deep chord inside.
I've always tried to make my life a liturgy,
the litany adds to the liturgical prayer.

The second psalm for Week 1 in the Hours
has always been a favorite,
although I have heard others complain about it.
It is the rhythm.

"Pray without ceasing," we are instructed.
A phrase that I never really understood until recently.
It should always be added that we
are not the ones who will be doing the praying.

It's hard to find words for when the Spirit
enters inside to make my life a prayer.
It is felt, it is "heard with the ears of your soul."
It is a treasure beyond price.

It's the only prayer I think
that quenches the thirst we have for our God.
Once tasted we are addicted in a good sense.
Like the Eucharist, we are One.

Eucharist means thanksgiving.

—

Pray Constantly

We are told this and read it.
But I have found it is not something I do.
It's something I don't do.
"Receive constantly," at least for me, says it best.

I have noticed when I stop doing,
there is an awareness there is prayer happening.
It happens through me.
It becomes conscious when I stop and recognize the Spirit.

St. Francis had the metaphor of a flute.
I am simply the instrument
through which the Spirit sings her praises.

It is truly humbling to find myself an instrument of the Spirit,
who chooses my body, heart, and soul as a means to worship,
even when unaware it is taking place.
It is a gift of pure grace.

A flute is hollow inside.
It is the musician using her breath to make the melody.
This is the best I can describe it.
Try to imagine the Spirit singing gratitude, grace, and humility.

If you can imagine these words being put to music,
that is what it sounds and feels like.
I can imagine no song being more glorious.

Spirit Prayer

Lately it seems I have lessened
my spiritual activities.
Not praying less,
but letting the Spirit do more than I ever could.

When the Spirit takes over my breathing,
it feels like being prepared to live
more in the other world.
The transport between them less a jolt.

There is a huge difference
when She is doing the praying.
I don't necessarily know what the prayer is for,
even what is said.

Surprisingly there is great comfort in this.
It's okay not to know.
The prayer is beyond me.
I know that I don't know.

It's yet one more surrender
to God who controls all things.
It is a blessing to turn all over to Him,
knowing He knows what is best.

This is another layer of trust
It feels like my life is no longer mine,
but in the best hands possible.
Are these holy words or really what is happening?

Yes. I deeply believe it is so.

—

When Prayer Does Not Come

There are nights of no prayer,
the spirit does not come,
and I am left to my own devices.
What happens is the emptiness turns to yearning.

Yearning has always seemed like absent presence to me.
If God wasn't experienced
then how would we know what we are yearning for?
(I have no idea if this has theological legs to stand on).

Sometimes I know it is the fault of my distractions.
Yet when the Spirit prays through me,
it seems clear the Spirit has power over the distractions.
It has power over my entire being.

All is pure gift of grace
and gratitude also has the power of the Spirit.
Perhaps they are one and the same.
I don't know.

Spirituality is like any knowledge.
The more you know,
the more you know you don't know.

And then the simplicity of it all drops you to your knees.

—

CHAPTER III

Grace

Grace Enters

John of the Cross talked of "purification,"
that must take place as we grow in
the spiritual life.
Jesus called it "pruning."

They are talking about the same growth process.
Our lives must be emptied, burned, pruned of
what blocks our union with God.
All that is not God is taken away.

Grace from God is the only way this is done.
John talked about the fire and the wood becoming one.
I feel it differently as I imagine we all do.
God knows best what will work for us.

I feel grace entering my entire being,
squeezing out all my impurities.
It is usually gentle yet driven by purpose.
I could not stop it if I wanted to.

I have already given my consent, so my free will
has joined with the will of God.
My mind and memory follow the will.
For me, it is the will that gives my yes.

I have given God my yes over and over again.
Sometimes it takes my breath away
as the grace enters my being
uniting me to Christ in mind, will, and spirit.

Sometimes it is gentle, sometimes forceful.
Why the difference, I don't know.
What I do know is the grace transforms me
in ways that I am sometimes conscious of.

—

Grace of Gratitude

Gratitude is perhaps the greatest of all graces.
It knows no boundaries
to be grateful for one thing is to be grateful
for all things.

It is centering, freeing, and the most liberating
for we are liberated from self.
what joy to be free
to think and love others instead of self.

To sing out in joy and praise
are the signs of gratitude.
humbling, ever so humbling.
Truly gift of pure grace!

It's a choice we can make
through the power of the spirit.
Sing out in joy and praise
truly gift of pure grace!

—

Pure Grace

Pure grace is a phrase that I use often,
but for the first time realize it is an oxymoron.
All grace is pure because its only source
is pure.

It was a vivid moment
when I realized I could never have
A pure motive to do anything.
There would always be at least a tinge of self-serving.

It was a vivid moment because it was a humbling moment.
Like everyone else I like to think that I am good.
Good is different from pure good.
Only Jesus and his mother managed that.

It's a good kind of humbling.
it frees me from trying to be someone I cannot be,
we teach our students to "do your best,"
trying to free them from the wounds of perfectionism.

Wounds that more of us carry than we should.
Put on us by others who are only trying to do their best
but destroying part of us in their expectations.
The Quakers used to purposely make a mistake
in their quilts since only God is perfect.

It makes me wonder if Quaker children are better adjusted.
I see children who are still in the state of pure grace.
Every fiber of their being is goodness and love.
And sadly those who carry the wounds of perfectionism.

Let us become like little children.
A phrase in scripture that has unpacked itself
in more ways than I could ever have imagined,
and continues to do so as I write my prayer.

—

Walking in Grace

Whenever I got up during my twelve-hour night,
the first thing that came to my consciousness
was that I was walking in grace.
It felt like I was walking on air.

It lasted for as long as the night lasted.
I could not try to replicate it for grace does not work that way,
but I could certainly remember it
with feelings of awe and wonder.

I did not even try to figure out what it meant
(I'm learning, I'm learning),
but accepted it for what it was,
pure gift of grace.

One of the things our Lady modeled for us
is that acceptance was the major part of her journey
to God, in God, and with God.
As Christ grew in her, she grew in Christ.

She walked in grace and lived in grace.
She accepted what came her way,
the gracious gifts and the suffering.
Gabriel promised her Christ would be her Son.

He didn't mention the crucifixion
and attacks on her chastity.
Like her Son, she taught us not to question grace
in whatever form it appears.

Walking in grace during the night
or suffering the attacks of the triggers.
God makes all things good.
We need only accept His protection of us.

—

What the Kingdom Feels Like

Why on earth did I just write these words?
What makes me think I can write this?
There is a desire/need to share with others,
with it comes the need to try.

Please know these words will not suffice.
Better you know that at the start.
I can tell you what it feels like to me.
It's the best I can do for now.

It feels like the greatest home I have ever known.
I am welcome there like no other place.
Entering in, I am filled with grace
that changes how I live my life.

The place exists in God,
so He is everywhere at the same time.
The communion of saints are the welcoming Body.
The mystical Body

I recognize people only by their essence at this time.
I do not know if it will be different later.
I suspect so.
"You cannot see the face of God and live."

It can be gentle like the past few days,
or so intense I am disoriented for days.
Those are hard and some come close to killing me,
so my son listens to me beg to stay and beg to stop.

The greatest recognition of being there is Grace.
Grace can rain on me or enter me gently.
I suppose it depends on what God sees I need.

It brings great trust, belief, and fidelity.
It is the belonging to something greater than me.
It brings a depth of gratitude
that goes deeper than I have ever known.

—

CHAPTER IV

Prayer

Authentic Prayer

Sometimes I used to pray
what my imagination or schooling
taught me that I should be praying.
It was far from authentic prayer.

It has been a long time since praying that way.
when keeping a journal we can write the same way—
what we think God wants to hear
or what we deeply need to say.

When teaching the journal class,
this point was sometimes an awakening
for some of the students.
What a joy it was to teach them otherwise.

Sometimes I am concerned of praying too much
from my feelings and thoughts.
Does He really want to know all this material?
If someone else asked, I would respond in the positive.

As in any love relationship, we care what the other person
is dealing with in daily life.
It is the power of a relationship to share this,
and most importantly, for the other person to listen.

God is always listening.
He has taught me this through years of talking
and his responses that He wants me to hear.
Not always what I want to hear but always grateful for truth.

Is there anything else we long for
more than to know that someone is always listening,
and that Person is always loving and caring?
He wants to hear what we have to say.

The most genuine way I know this is true,
because of the tears that fall
when finding that He has listened and responded.
It's the greatest gift of grace there is.

He wants to hear what we have to say.
He already knows it,
but it makes a difference how we say what we have to say.
It's important we speak.

—

Being Becoming Prayer

What is it that turns my being into prayer?
Of course the answer is God, but when?
I suspect when the devastation of people and land
become much too much for me to process in prayer.

What is happening in Texas, the Caribbean, and Florida
is too overwhelming and leaves me helpless to just pray…
there are still wars ravaging people into refugees.
There is part of me glued to the television in order to know to pray.

Then it is time to turn off the TV and turn to the solitude
in my quiet, well-protected home.
It is not for me to smugly enjoy my safety.
My safety is connected to the safety of all others.

But it is a gift of quiet where I can pull these people
in real time into my heart and soul.
The fear for them is real,
the tears come from being overwhelmed in our common humanity.

There is no helplessness when I turn to prayer.
Prayer when I know our Father is paying attention.
By making my being prayer,
He unites myself into Him, and we both pay attention.

Others could read this as just words,
but it is written through His Heart and Soul
where He calls me into His Being
to join with Him to do my part.

—

Birthday Celebrations

Birthdays aren't really about cake and ice cream.
Birthdays are for celebrating the life of a
loved one

Being children of God,
it is a time for looking at ourselves
to really study the image of him we were created in.
What about us reflects the image of God?

For every single one of us, it will be different,
that is what makes it a reverent process.
No two of us are alike.
Yet we all present an aspect of God.

This will be a humbling process if we are honest,
and we must be honest
this is our gift to God
for making us who we are.

So amid the celebrations, presents, and cards,
we must find time for prayer
to find out how he truly made us in his image.
and then we must live what we discover.

Prayer is not our usual plan to celebrate a birthday,
but if you think it through it is probably
the most important part of our day.
a new tradition to keep.

—

Back Again

In these times when my thoughts, feelings, and prayers
are all over the spiritual maps,
it sometimes takes me time to remember
my Centering Prayer.

Not the sitting quiet and turning over the
thoughts into silence, into mysterious prayer.
I mean the prayer that pulls me out of disorientation
into my life being centered in Christ.

It is always the prayer and state of being in gratitude.
It pulls me out of my selfishness
into the world of my brothers and sisters.
Grateful for my condo, I pray desperately for the homeless.

I pray for those who really suffer:
those in any kind of pain and doubt and those alone.
The world quiets again in God's order, not mine.

It is Christ's Kingdom, His work, His call.
Answering Him with a yes, he takes it seriously,
even when I don't. Especially when I don't
He patiently waits for me to return, even when
I don't know where I have gone.
He waits and then lets me know that I had left.

I went into me and not with Him.
He's okay with us going into ourselves,
but not by ourselves. Never by ourselves.
He never leaves our side even when we leave His.

That is what being God means.

Create a Clean Heart

"Create a clean heart in me, O Lord."
The psalmists had their finger on the pulse of the faith.
They knew it would take the Lord, and only the Lord,
to create a clean heart in them.

Why did I hear this line as soon as my eyes closed tonight?
The fervor that accompanied it was intense and sincere.
At some level, the Spirit is telling me that I need
a clean heart within me.

It feels like it is not just a nightly prayer
for tonight only.
There is a sense that it is a prayer to be prayed
over time.

Maybe it is a theme for the summer or the retreat.
I do not know. Only that it has surfaced
with deep desire attached to it.
The longing gives me a clue to its importance.

A clean heart suggests to me a heart that is pure in intention.
There is no guile, no personal agenda,
a heart filled with nothing but love for the Lord.
Is that possible this side of death?

I truly do not know,
but I do know the desire to have a clean heart is genuine.
I doubt we can ever judge the purity of our heart,
but we can want to have it for the love of God.

—

Discernment

Gift of Ignatius
gift from the Jesuits.
The guidance to discover
whose spirit is moving within our hearts and souls.

Do we worship at the altar of God
or get lost and march under Satan's banner?
The former brings peace, acceptance, and
agitation if necessary to move us.
The latter brings fear, anxiety, and agitation for the sake of agitation.

We must always be discerning where we worship.
God is the center of our worship of Him.
we love, desire, and burn with our love for Him.
Jesus is the focus of our thoughts, feelings, and actions.

Evil has a subtle way of making ourselves
the center of our worship.
Our fear, anxiety, and self become the focus.
The gift of discernment helps us to recognize
and take action to what is happening.

Evil can be very subtle,
which makes it all so heinous.
It is why we need the rules of discernment,
and an objective spiritual director or friend.

Fr. Toner, S.J., taught us to get angry, instead of fearful of evil.
The anger pulls us out of our victimization,
(I name that out of personal experience)
to reclaim our identity as sons or daughters of Christ.

Secure in our identity as a child of God,
we have the power to banish evil
back to where it came, in order to spend our time and energy
adoring He who created us to be His.

—

God of Gentleness, God of Love

Love me slowly.
Love me gently.
But please do love me.

The pages I have written you,
the tears cried,
the anguish and despair
You hear.

I begged You to answer and guide me,
only to shamefully discover my fear of hearing you.
Please open my fearful heart and mind.
Turn mistrust into trust.
Simple words.
Heart-wrenching change in perception

When you make demands, I hear.
When you want or take away, I surrender.
When you want to give, I run away.

Please take away the fight in me.
Help me to stop.
Help me to listen.

Your only weapon is love,
more powerful than my own weapons of fear.
Your love stronger than my fear of abandonment.
My mistrust crumbles in the face of Your belief.
Your presence gentle in its demand I face you.
And see you.
And begin to open up to you.
My weapons you have taken away,
for they are no longer needed.

Your light pulls me out of my darkness
and there is nowhere to run
they damaged their eyesight.

Love me slowly,
Love me gently,
But please do love me.

Just Be

"My Lord and my God."
Breathing in the Spirit, breathing out impurities.
We seem to best connect
when the prayer is the most simple.

Why am I discovering this now?
What does this mean about You?
You who described Yourself simply as "I Am."
You said all that you needed to say to describe Yourself.

How do I describe myself to you?
"I am here."
It seems to say all I need to say to you
about me.

I am here,
for you to send, love, adore you, and just be.
Just be.
Waiting upon your presence for whatever you wish.

Your answers to me are as simple as my questions.
"Who are you?"
"What is it you would have me do or be?"
Just be.

Just be is what you answer the most.
In just being, I am here.
waiting, vulnerable, adoring.
I am here.

Learning to Just Be before Doing

Being rather than doing
is so contrary to our Western minds.
Not trying to "do" sounds like laziness and sloth.
It goes against every fiber of our being.

But if we do not know how to just be,
how will we even know what God wants us to do?
And if we don't know how to be,
how will we know who we are?

It was through learning how to be
that I learned who I was.
I wasn't just mother, teacher,
counselor, and spiritual director.

Those were important roles I took on in life,
and I firmly believe that is what God wanted me to do.
But more than what he wanted me to do,
He wanted me to be his beloved daughter.

Why?
What parent does not want their child
to first know how special and loved they are?
All the more so with God and we, his children.

To what purpose?
That's just it—to no purpose.
Just to be
who he created us to be.

Long Empty Days

These are the hardest of days.
It's okay if there is nothing going on outside,
but when there is nothing going on inside
it's hard to find purpose in just being.

When prayer is taking place,
there is a joy and honor to be God's instrument.
When that prayer is not happening,
I can only wait.

It's hard not to ask, "What am I doing wrong?"
But that is not fair
because I wasn't doing anything right
when prayer was happening all the time.

It brings me to waiting…and feelings.
Just because I don't feel it does not mean
prayer is not happening.
It takes faith and grace to live this belief.

From all that has gone on lately,
I believe that my being is my prayer.
Feelings or no feelings.
Is that arrogant?

Maybe it's humility, not arrogance,
to believe that God works beyond our limited
set of feelings and consciousness.
It is believing God is the center and not us.

God does not need for us to know
whether or not He is active within us.
The audacity to think we must know
is to put ourselves in His place.

He is the Creator
we are the creature.
Yes, He raises us up to be His adopted children.
That makes us heirs.

This is the only way to remain centered in truth.

Night Prayer

When the lights go out, the prayer dives deeper
into the warmth and solace of the dark and solitude.
He wraps me in his arms
to let me know I am never alone in prayer.

There is such a comfort in this movement,
and I am enjoying the gift and company.
There is a sense Jesus is teaching me how
to pray to our Father.

The whole image of Father
has had to go through many changes for me to relate.
The most recent change is now I always see Him
as the prodigal son's father.

That has made a difference in prayer.
Just writing the Father and the prodigal son's father
make a difference to me, although they cannot be different
"And God still be God" (KRK)

So I look forward to turning out the lights each night.
Never have I been a person who falls right to sleep.
Instead of churning things through my head,
the time is spent in the gift of prayer.
Amen.

Our Bodies as a Living Sacrifice.

Perhaps I am understanding this completely wrong,
but an experience last week gave this saying new meaning.
It was when praying that my body became prayer.
My body became a living prayer.

I can't really call it a sacrifice,
except it consumed what was happening
and what I was doing.
It was an honor, more than what I think of sacrifice.

Is there anything that I can give up?
Perhaps my wants and desires.
But what more could I desire than to be
Living prayer?

I think of the crosses in my life and wonder
if they are what allowed me to become prayer.
The crosses were real, and I carried them
through some horrific times.

Those experiences certainly left me changed.
Compassion and empathy were more developed.
Understanding for where others are coming from deepened.
I stopped using my ruler to judge others and looked at their rulers.

The people who have been my teachers have changed me.
The experience of being understood and valued
taught me the importance of giving that gift to others.

Postures of Prayer

Very often writing is my prayer.
The words are a gift, and I do not know
ahead of time what will be written.
It's written as it is typed.

Other times the Spirit prays through me
with intense desires, feelings, imagination, and insights.
St. Paul gives us the gift of words to describe this:
"the Spirit is groaning within us."

At the end of every retreat,
the gratitude and desire to give myself to Christ
are so great that I find myself prostrate on the floor
in front of the altar.

There is the need to respond in some bodily manner.
Sometimes in my room at home,
the depth finds me in the Muslim prayer position.
On my knees with forehead touching the ground.

On pilgrimage and on Manresa's sacred grounds
I find myself touching and almost holding onto a special place.
There are times when the only response is
to fall on my knees.

It only makes sense that when we are so overtaken
in prayer that we have a need to act on it
in a physical manner.
We engage body, mind, and spirit.

Like the writing, I do not know ahead of time
when I will fall into these types of position.
It happens by instinct
and the feelings are that of wholeness.

And I am grateful.

Praying the News

There is a new sense of mission in praying for peace.
I can pray for peace with my head in the sand
or watch the news and know where and how
to direct my prayers more accurately.

These are my brothers, sisters, and children who are
fleeing from their homes, just wanting to stay alive.
But the agents of terror are also my
brothers and sisters.

How do I reconcile that in prayer?
I can only think they need the most prayer
because they are blind to the evil they are promoting,
the suffering they are causing.

This is so hard, but we are all God's children.
By watching the news, I have names, countries, and acts
to direct the prayers of my heart.
Intimacy with Christ is not blind love.

Being in love means standing at the foot of the cross.
It means watching and hearing His actions and words.
Intimacy means "being with."
in His glory and when He weeps.

Sanctus Chimes

The chimes on my deck have been singing a lot.
It made me think of the Sanctus bells from the mass years ago.
They were rung just before the consecration.
I always thought they were saying "Pay attention."

The chimes are saying the same thing.
There is so much to pay attention to.
The Lord's presence is always consecrating
our earth, nature, and lives.

"Focus," the bells always reminded me.
The same is true of the chimes.
Focus on the Lord's presence,
pay attention to how He is working here and now.

Notice for instance the daily changes in the trail.
During the last couple of days
the wildflowers have been popping up,
their fragrance adding delightful aroma.

Focus on how the Spirit is moving you closer to Christ,
through beauty, gratitude, and awe.
Meditate on the writings the Spirit sends.
Reflect on the gift of children and grandchildren.

The sound of chimes is a gentle sound,
breaking any silence with just a whisper of enchantment.
They now also have a sacred call,
as did the Sanctus bells in years past.

Take and Receive

Derived from Ignatian Suscipe

"Take, Lord, and receive all my liberty"
For you, Jesus, have claimed me as your own.
Freedom I have found only in surrender.
Your name called mine in baptism.
Your Father becomes my Father.

"My memory"
You have redeemed and healed.
You brought the shamed, smashed child I had hidden so deeply,
into Your light where you breathed life into my deepest wounds.
Your forgiveness becomes my forgiveness,
as I reclaim the gift of my heritage.

"My understanding"
Now consecrates the present as you teach me to understand
You are discovered in the daily, in the ordinary.
You ask me to be your passion, your compassion for others.
Your kingdom becomes my home.

"My entire will"
Please take, Lord,
for how could I want other than what you want
and still live in you?
Be in love with you?
Hope in you?
My will exists only in your will.

"All I love and possess"
Carry no meaning outside of your purpose for me.
Only in following your call do I find value and substance.
To you, Lord, I return it."

"Give me only your love,"
So that I may love as you call me to love
as you have loved me.
May my love radiate from the sacred center of your heart.
"That is enough for me."

"Give me your grace"
To search, to hunger
to pray and be your prayer for all others.
Your grace has freed me to love for you.
Your life becomes my life.

That is all I want to be.
"Take, Lord, and receive."

The World Looks Different

While reading a book, I glanced out the window
and did a double take.
The colors were more defined—the browns browner
and the greens greener.

The shape of the trees were more defined
as was each branch.
It was a new clarity, which made
for the double take.

What I see deeper is His creation
and what he has gifted us with so graciously.
He wants us to be truly delighted with His gifts.

I love the "principle and foundation"
for Ignatius makes the point about the gift.
It is pure gift, and in its purity,
it leads us straight back to God.

I remember wishing once to be a tree,
because my very being would be an act of adoration to God.
It's been a lot of years since then,
but I now know my being is life in adoration to God.

It's all His pure gift.

Transforming Presence of God

God's felt presence causes deep transformation.
It happens all at once.
It is understood much slower.
There is so much that happens.

There is surrender to His will
and abandonment into his heart.
The self-interest is gone and replaced
by much liberation.

What does he want?
It depends.
Sometimes nothing,
sometimes everything.

I suspect it depends on the condition he finds me.
If there is something to give, he accepts it.
If there is nothing inside, he accepts the nothing.
He understands those times.

His presence is sometimes a surprise.
There is no prior prayer, no asking.
Suddenly I am aware He is with me,
giving, always giving.

It's hard to accept that sometimes He just wants the company.
He doesn't need me,
but that does not stop him from wanting,
and so He makes his presence known.

It's beyond my comprehension,
so he does what he needs to do with this daughter.
He tells me to just let it be.
That is all I need for now.

Waiting at the Doorway

Sitting on the doorstep
of yet another one of the rooms
"I have prepared for you in my Father's house,"
a new attitude becalms me.

Is it the age of wisdom that assures me to wait patiently?
Or is it the fear of the child warning,
"do not ask for what is beyond you."

He has brought me here, of this I am sure.
To learn that thresholds are for more than waiting.
It is not my place to knock nor peer inside.

I came searching for Christ.
To know
To serve
To abide with in loving mystery.

But I find the door is not made of metal or wood,
but a mirror that reflects, disciplines,
and demands more surrendering.

As I ponder, look, and struggle to learn,
I remember once more that my pastor always says,
"One must learn to see with the eyes of the soul."

What is a doorway?
Is it a barrier or an entryway?
I cannot say yet.
I do not know.

CHAPTER V

Silence and Solitude

A Day without Prayer

The end of the day can come and if
I have not prayed, there is an intense restlessness.
The day cannot end—no matter how tired.
Missing prayer no longer is an option.

That makes it the most important part of the day.
Being a night person, prayer is my closing act.
No longer do written prayers by others suffice,
it needs to be communication between God and myself.

Our best conversations take place in silence.
A simple uniting of mind, heart, and will.
A day without prayer is a day without love.
And that just can't be.

—

A Glorious Fall Day

Today I reached the soccer field an hour before game time.
As I was the only one there, it was natural prayer began
as I arrived into the silence and solitude.
The almost full moon was showing at 4:00 p.m.

It gets harder and harder to describe the silence.
It felt like the fall trees wrapped me into their prayer of being.
It was not possible to be in that space and not pray.
The weather, trees, and moon were shouting of God.

There is nothing to do in these times
except to be still.
The creation of the Creator
sings His praises.

One only need be still to hear the choir singing.
It rejoices in its beauty and fullness.
I am but a small part of His creation.

To be but a small part in this miracle
is a gift to be cherished
and not forgotten.
His Presence is like surround sound.

"For those to have eyes to see, see
and those who have ears to hear, hear."

—

A Single Flame

Today has been a very quiet one
and nothing came to mind until going downstairs.
I noticed a simple, single flame
burning inside of me.

It is much more quiet and gentle
than the medieval liturgy from the other day.
I thought of the eternal flame keeping watch
by the grave of JFK.

That is what it most feels like,
a flame that is keeping watch.
It seems appropriate for Lent
as I wait to see how the Spirit will work within me.

The flame, for as small as it is,
consumes me with the fire of desire
that this Lent deeply makes my being
an instrument of quiet adoration.

Life, prayer, and discernment take on such different meanings,
knowing that I don't do it.
It makes me think of those on vigil
waiting to meet the bridegroom.

Advent is waiting in pregnant expectation for new life.
Lent feels like a much quieter vigil waiting for salvation.
The center of both is Jesus.
Jesus, the center of my everything.

I love and cherish the quiet.
The time of waiting is made sacred by the Light.
Thank you.

I Am Here

Three silent words still sound
as they did the other night.
It reminds me of "I AM."
In two words, He said all there was to say.

"I am here" gives a sense of union and protection,
in that no matter where I am
or what I am doing,
He is with me and wants me to know.

It is another gift of pure grace.
That He is everywhere I know in my intellect.
Hearing Him say the words,
I feel in my heart.

It makes me realize how much
I still walk around with some fear of life
even though so much of it has been healed.
It manifests in shyness and introversion.

It's something I have lived with all my life.
It's difficult being in groups, crowds, and especially strangers.
Self-worth is challenged.
God knows this and breaks through with grace.

God knows me and what I need.
Could there be any greater blessing
than to be known and protected
by my Creator and the protectors He sends?

"I Am Here."

—

Inner Tabernacle

There are nights that I close my eyes and
then remember "Night Prayer."
There are nights that I do not then pick up the book to pray.

Those are the nights that I am already
resting in our sacred chamber.
It feels like we are one protected in a glass chamber,
and words would only hit the glass and would not penetrate,
despite their beauty, depth, and sacredness.

I live alone, and there is very little noise; few words, if any.
People may think that is solitude.
It's not.

I can't make solitude happen, even in the
silence of my days and nights.
It comes to me.
It is easily discernable from the silence
because it is rich and filled with the Spirit.

It is filled with the presence of God
so different from the ordinary quiet.
"Rest in the Lord," I hear my director's words.

In the quiet, my focus is all over the place.
But in the solitude, my focus is Christ.
There are no rights or wrongs to worry about.
It's not my performance.

It is Christ's movement, and He takes me up into it.
I simply need to be.

"Just be yourself," the Olympic commentators continually repeat.
In prayer I can only be myself.
He accepts no other.

It is true rest from a lifetime of being
who the church told me I should be.
Sometimes stirring unrest and inner conflict.

The answers, rest, and truth
come in the solitude.
When it comes.

—

Interior Prayer

Prayer is not summoning God.
"Summon," meaning "to call or bring over."
Vocal community prayer is addressing God.
Silent prayer is diving deep within.

There are many different types of prayer,
all emanating from the Spirit.
It is God summoning us to prayer
and sometimes calling us to enter Him within ourselves.

The movement is so gentle and quiet,
the only activity is the silence.
It is God calling Himself,
looking at Himself within our very soul.

It's not hard to miss because the silence moves
a person to the deepest point within,
the inner tabernacle inside
where He resides at all times.

It's true it's a very noisy world,
and sometimes the loudest noise is inside.
But when God wants to get our attention,
He makes sure the silence is louder than the noise.

The relief from the noise is pure restfulness.
The grace protects our soul from the terror of the noise.
It is a consolation that is difficult to describe.
When you hear His call—follow.

—

Middle of the Night Moonlight

It's three in the morning,
but the moonlight is too captivating to sleep.
Its serene light captures
the serenity of God within.

It casts its mystical light over the earth,
promising that its Creator
gives the same mystical and gentle light
to those who can see.

It's a time for prayer.
Not the prayer of my words and wishes,
but the prayer that comes from
the light casting its glow upon us.

Moonlight is much gentler than sunlight.
It does not burn. It is as gentle as its rays
cast its light on those awake and asleep.
It falls gently on the earth,

They say the moon affects the tides.
They also say it affects the water within us.
I do not know about such things.
All I know is the serenity it brings in its gentleness.

It is time to sleep,
but I am grateful for this time of prayer
in the moonlight tonight.
I love sleeping under its healing light.

—

Night Rain

The night rain adds nourishment to the silence.
Prayer can be called nourishment
for our thirst for God
is quenched and filled like a dry sponge.

The combination of night rain in prayer
reminds me of the earth's dependence
on God for our growth, our existence.
We can't live long without water.

When I hear rain, I hear God.
When I hear rain in the solitude
I hear the God who provides us life.
He is nourishing me now into another understanding of life.

God gives life to all and in probably a different
way for each individual.
He knows our needs—
we were created in His image.

It is pouring outside
and I feel a direct correlation.
It has been pouring inside for months now.
Grace has been raining in and pouring over onto paper.

I am deeply blessed and grateful.

—

Painful Noise

Noise can cause physical and emotional suffering.
That is certainly a melodramatic statement,
but it has become one of my truths.
As quiet can be healing, noise can cause pain.

It can be the noise from the outside or inside.
Whatever interferes with the silence
is an obstruction to divine union.

Silence of union can be found in the midst of a crowd.
Obstruction to the silence can be found
while alone in my room.

The gift of silence has been growing exponentially
these last six months.
Studies have shown that prolonged abuse alters the brain.
I am wondering if prolonged silence alters something inside.

As Jesus has called me deeper into Him,
there is a new vulnerability that comes with deeper love.
The environment of that love is silence,
and there is a growing sensitivity to the harm noise causes.

It feels like I need the silence to be,
as I need the air to breathe.
Both seem equally necessary.
At least both are necessary in my present life.

God provides what we need.
Yes, it hurts at times in the noise,
but as David knows when I need him,
Christ knows when the silence is necessary.

And I am grateful.

—

Prayer Nights

There are nights when God keeps me up.
"It feels like…He wants my company.
Do I dare write that… I remember in joy
all the nights I long for His company.

As with all my prayer lately,
there is nothing for me to do.
Just be,
with him.

Words mean absolutely nothing.
Talking seems disrespectful.
Company—more meaningful than presence.
Companionship seems greater in silence.

Feelings spoken in silence seem deeper,
silent communication is more reverent.
There is more majesty
for this is sacred ground.

More paradox…
Words spoken would be less profound.
Love passed in silence more everlasting.
There is no end to the Being of God.

It then has to be an eternity
discovering our God
who chooses an eternity
to love us into him

Silence

Silence is much more than the absence of noise,
even if physically quiet, we still have our
minds making loud sounds.
Silence is a gift of grace.
Holy silence we can actually hear.

In the grace of silence we know the presence of God.
We can't make it happen by ourselves.
It is a gift.
It is presence and peace and calls for active passivity.

This active passivity is not easy.
We must wait for our minds to clear
and empty ourselves in order to receive.
There can be restlessness in the waiting.

It takes great patience not to give up and walk away.
For me, it is always like going through a dark tunnel
during which I often pace, recognizing it is coming.
The gift is then emergence into the silence.

It is a silence that we savor;
if we remain within the silence,
we are moved into solitude
and experience our oneness with God.

Our only response is praise and gratitude,
which all happens silently in the solitude.

Stillness and Silence

Stillness is a different kind of silence.
God sometimes uses His silence to speak.
We can learn about Him in silence.
In stillness, we come in contact with "I Am."

It feels like we learn in the silence
what God wants to teach us about Himself.
"I Am" is stillness where God is "Being."
"I Am Who I Am."

In my heart, there is the feeling of a child in wonder,
kneeling at the feet of "I Am".
The words "awe" and "wonder" do not begin to tell the story.
There is no story to "I Am."

Reverential adoration while on my knees
is my only possible response in the stillness of "I Am."
Instinctively I know not to look up.
"You cannot see the face of God and live."

Trembling quakes through my body,
a trembling that I can neither name as good or bad.
It is a natural physical reaction
to being in the presence of "I Am."

—

Too Silent for Words

There comes a time when the silence
can no longer be talked about.
It's somewhat of a paradox…

It's frustrating to have no words.
The writing is my prayer and provides release and expression.
On the other hand,
the silence is so beautiful.

It's a gift of pure grace just to be immersed in Him.
In the silence.
In the sacredness.
There are no similes.

Tonight there will be no more writing.
It is quieter than silence.
Amen.

—

Chambers of Silence

Of all the different types of silence,
there is one I can only label as
"extremely uncomfortable."
for that is what it feels like…at best.

There is no noise that fills it,
no noise that eases it.
In fact, any sounds seem
only to aggravate it.
So I turn off my favorite music
and hope all outside noise stays away.

How do you describe something that is so empty?
Yet it does seem to have a life of its own.
It is active in its emptying,
and that is what hurts.

It burrows away on the inside
hollowing out chamber after chamber.
As they ring out,
the silence echoes even deeper.

I cannot fill it.
it leaves me totally helpless
and on the edge anticipating.
It can't be run away from or slept through.

It demands I remain on that edge,
feeling and listening.

Feeling helpless,
listening to emptiness.
Try not anger, questions, or even writing.

It tolerates only tears.
Silent ones of course.

CHAPTER VI

Mystery

"Do You Know What I Have Done for You?"

When you ask this of me, all I want to do is kneel at your feet,
put my head to the ground, and promise you that I do.
This past year I have filled two notebooks
writing all that you have done for me and continue to do.

The unworthiness is not false humility.
You have spoiled me quite extensively
and I'm aware of gifts of grace
and probably not aware of many others.

You washed the feet of the apostles,
making the Messiah the servant of others.
Making all your disciples, then and now,
the servant of others.

I feel that in giving spiritual direction,
but I am lacking in much else.
Retirement is not so bad now that I accept
the contemplative lifestyle I have adopted.

To be perfectly honest, I have adopted no lifestyle;
it has adopted me.
I understand it is God's will for me
and no longer fight it.

Why do we resist and do mental gymnastics
to avoid the only thing that will truly give us joy?
God has a will for each of us, and He wants our happiness.
I can look back on all the movements of
my life and not be surprised.

"God has special plans for you,"
my guidance counselor told me at age fifteen.
I was relieved it was not to be a nun for I wanted children
but thrilled to find He wanted me all along.

—

Endless Consolation

Perhaps what makes consolation, consolation,
is it feels like it is endless,
even though Ignatius warned us otherwise.
But the endlessness can mean something other than time.

It seems that every time I turn to prayer,
Christ is there patiently waiting for me.
His patience seems endless.
He always seems to be there lately.

The consolation is endless
because God and his love are without end.
There is no bottom to His love.
It is our human condition that puts limits to it.

Sometimes in His generosity
He will remove those limits for a second or two,
and there is a glimpse into the divine mystery.
A gift of pure grace that cannot be withstood for long.

Such a glimpse changes me.
I want to serve and surrender my life into His.
As this continues, I start to recognize His Presence
more often during the day.

Some would call them just coincidence.
But they seem to be clear affirmations
that are gifts from Him,
I am grateful they come from the all-knowing Being.

—

Eucharist

Of all the consolations, graces, and miracles,
the greatest of all of these is the Eucharist.
He gave all of Himself to us.
He died and rose again for His love of the Father and us.

"What does this mean for us today?"
Our pastor used to ask at most of his homilies.
That could take most of eternity to answer…

Eucharist is all of the above
consolation, grace, and miracle.
I hate to overuse this phrase,
but my heart leaps as did John in his mother's womb.

Earth is essentially our womb
before our birth into resurrected life.
So it makes sense that at receiving the Body of Christ,
we too would leap in our womb upon meeting Him.

As did John, we recognize our Savior
and leap with joy whenever and wherever we meet.
I'm sure the prodigal son's father was leaping with joy
seeing his son coming in the distance.

We leap when we experience joy,
and what better word is there for communion
than joy?
A miracle taking place in our presence.

The only appropriate response
is to leap in the air in joy.
We become like the little children
He instructed us to become, and we happily do so.

—

Flaming Color

Why do leaves turn into flaming orange and red
right before their death?
Are we supposed to be that way—
before our death we turn our brightest?

If we have been on the purgation road,
it might make sense.
Our impurities are so burned out of us
we are left with a luminous glow.

Yet so many people seem to be the opposite.
As they age, they become withdrawn and hidden.
What does God want?
Probably not how our culture deals with the aging.

I would take a guess that He wants us
wearing our wisdom like Joseph's colored coat.
Our contemplation like the royal diadem.
Our silence would sound like the court trumpets.

If we compare ourselves to the leaves in their dying,
maybe we have to rethink what God wants of us,
instead of what our culture expects.
What a glorious paradigm shift that would be.

—

Heart of Compassion

Mary, John, and the others
need shift ever so slightly to include me.
"You belong here with us,"
their eyes speak briefly in the silence,
and their eyes then focus back to the cross.

Trembling with fear, I follow their gaze
and find it is the love in his eyes
that now trembles through me.

The violence that tears his flesh
opens my heart so to join in his.
Instead of anger I find compassion,
and forgiveness instead of hate.

How can any of this make sense?
Somehow it does, but please don't ask.

In the dark shadow of the cross,
He gives me comfort.
In place of fear, safety.
Compassion flows from his heart into mine
and out again.

"What you have asked for
is now given."
"You are to spend this for me,
in my name."

Indwelling

Thank you, Abba, for coming and
making your home in me.
This is something you promised,
and I am grateful You make me conscious of Your presence.

"The Father and I will come and make our home in you."
You made a covenant with us, and you
are our God who keeps His promises,
and we are Your people.

What kind of God dwells inside His creatures?
Only a God who is love,
and as love has chosen us.
We have not chosen you, but we say our yes to you.

Our yes to you is our daily prayer.
As we receive our daily bread from you,
we consecrate our lives to you each day,
remembering, "You are our God, and we are Your people."

Your presence is gentle but so alive.
It is way past time to sleep,
and I must not be greedy with your gifts.
I pray that you will allow me to fall asleep in you.

—

Infinite Depth

When God summons us deep inside ourselves
to be with him in His mystery,
we can sometimes become disoriented.
We need "decompression chambers" like the professionals.

There is no ocean floor,
no place that tells us we have plumbed
to the deepest depth possible.
Because there is no floor or deepest depth.

God is infinite in His mystery.
We will spend eternity plunging into his midst
and never reach the end.
Something we cannot understand, only accept.

This is what my son is doing.
He does not need a compression chamber like I do.
He can travel back and forth
in order to give me a taste of the infinite.

I understand that I don't understand
and that is enough.
"I do not seek things that are too lofty for me."
I believe in mystery. I believe in David.

It is enough for me.

—

Knowing and Not Knowing

It is true there are things that I just know.
But the more God reveals,
the same standard follows about all knowledge:
"The more you know, the more you know you don't know."

God has revealed much about my son, the kingdom,
grace, love, gratitude, fidelity, adoration, and fervor.
We are made in His image,
and He created us for love.

With all that He has revealed,
it is like getting a three-second vision and experience of these things.
So I know, but I also know each is an abyss
that will take eternity to plumb its depths.

—

St. Paul

We all owe St. Paul our gratitude
for finding the words that explain spiritual experiences.
"It is no longer I who live,
but Christ who lives in me."

Paul's words came to me last night
while struggling to find words to fit what was happening.
What was happening was it was no longer
I who was breathing, but Christ breathing in me.

It's being lost in Christ
but without loss of identity.
We are one,
yet Christ is Christ and Denise is Denise.

Once this is experienced,
the mystical body becomes more clear.
It is not Christ and me,
but Christ and his creation.

We are all brothers and sisters living in love.
As St. Paul said,
"Love is patient, love is kind…"
We don't become saints for "I still do the
things I do not want to do."

But we are now aware of what living in the kingdom means.
We are given the clarity on how we ought to live.
However, knowing and doing are not the same thing.
Like St. Paul, we all will the one thing but can't always do it.

The prodigal son's Father knows this, and we are forgiven
before we begin the long trek home with speech prepared.
Christ does not want our "sacrifices and burnt offerings."
Our being open to receiving Him is His desire.

We need each other on this journey.
We don't go at it alone.
Let us all will the one thing
traveling together as pilgrims on this adventure home.

—

Tears

St. Ignatius coined the phrase "the gift of tears."
He and St. Francis cried so often in love
they both damaged their eyesight.

It's hard to explain what happened the other night
when I could not stop crying.
There were two things I remember:
crying over vulnerability and wanting to go home.

Maybe they are one and the same.
Maybe my director can explain.
Please don't judge me—
I know the selfishness contained in the feelings.

A few years ago, there was an experience from David
that I could only call "creation."
It was blinding light and love that, if it continued,
would have obliterated me.

Yet I begged my son and mother to allow me to stay,
knowing full well the answer would be "Not now."
The other night Michael Buble sang the song,
"I want to go home," and the tears would not stop.

I know whatever work I have left to do is undone,
or I would not still be here.

I know I have not loved enough here,
and the vulnerability that brings runs deep.
I usually call it "being turned inside out."
Forgive my lack of having the right words.

The tears are not sad, nor are they joyful.
They are tears of longing and love.
I know the "alleluia days are coming."
Please just allow me to be wherever it is I am.

—

Unknowing

Living in a world of unknowing
is learning how to trust
in He who knows all
and wills what is best for me.

Many questions start to surface,
but they are filled with wanting to know,
wanting the control,
wanting to direct my life according to my will, not His.

This is not who I want to be—
someone who insanely believes I have the control.
What I do feel is okay to ask for
is reassurance and support.

Someone reading the writings may ask,
"Why on earth do you need reassurance?"
It's because they seem to be going deeper,
and yesterday the writing felt like it was over my head.

Being so deeply in love is both humbling and exciting.
It is tremendous vulnerability to let go of my entire self
and hand it over to another.
But since it is handing over to Jesus, there is wholeness.

This is not a new movement; it has happened countless other times.
Each time it has felt like giving the very depth of my soul.
This is the same, only God keeps burrowing deeper and deeper.
How long can this go on?

I have used the expression "being turned inside out" before.
It is like turning a purse or pocket inside
out so there is nothing left inside.
Until He comes to fill it.

—

Who Do You Say That I Am?

This is a question that is often on my mind,
but I am doing the asking.
"Who are you?"
I continuously want to ask!

Who are you?
You, who consume my desire and longing?
You, who bring me exaltation and healing?
You, who are invisible and yet so present?

I have experienced your miracles in my life.
My heart has come close to exploding my human limits
when filled with your divine love.
You, who have taught me to live the kingdom values.

You have allowed me to drown in the darkness
of what seems to be your absence
and experience temptations of evil trying
to make me doubt your being.

During those times, I cling to faith,
which is a gift of the Spirit.
I rely on my memories of all the times
you have been with me beyond all doubt.

This is at once both a tumultuous journey
and one of peace that the world cannot give.
It is a pilgrimage visiting unknown places,

Yet you ask me, "Who am I?"
What word out of all the words do I use
to describe your omnipotence?
Mary's resonates within "Rabboni."

My Lord and my God.

—6/

CHAPTER VII

Trust

Alabaster Jar

The jar had to be broken
to fulfill her burning desire.
Desire to express the depth of her love for him.
This mattered more to her than anything else.

More than the risk of entering into another's home,
uninvited, unwanted, defying all convention.
Risking rejection and shame,
desire drove her actions.

She was the precious perfume in the jar.

Her love was total,
but all of her could not be given
until first being broken.
Her being had to be freed from where it was contained.

We hunger and strive for wholeness,
yet he loves us in our brokenness.
Sometimes it is called "purification,"
a strange name for something so painful.

We cannot enter into him
with our masks and disguise of self-sufficiency.
We must be broken down to our naked helplessness.
It is then he can call us into his being.

Later he knelt at the feet of his disciples.
He too poured liquid on their feet
as a sign of great love,
calling them to serve as he served.

None of this makes any sense
unless you have known his love.
Then it makes all the sense in the world.
How can we not want to do what he did?

To be who he is!

We must be broken first.
How else would we know it is he, not us.
It is not even our prayer to pray,
only our prayer to receive.

Trusting God's Prayer In Us

There are times God tolerates no verbal prayer,
the noise of my voice becomes a distraction, rather than sacred.
It is disconcerting to say the least.
He wants not the words of my mouth, but my heart.

There are times he lets me know he owns my heart.
He only wants prayer from my core of silence.
There are other times he just, "shushes" my thoughts.

He determines the manner of my prayer.
He simply takes it out of my hands,
by substituting his prayer for mine.

—

Night Sky Connection

Today I felt totally disconnected from You.
It was busy, and there were painters here when I came home.
It all left me discombobulated.
Disconnected from you left me confused.

The confusion made me realize how deeply
we have been so connected for these months
at the feeling and reality level.
I have become dependent upon our oneness.

When we are one, life has a tone of deep, quiet joy.
I face the ups and downs of life not quite the same.
Unlike the balloon let loose going anywhere,
I am grounded at the deepest level in your love.

That was not present today and caused some angst.
It left me feeling like the balloon,
grounded nowhere and flying in different directions.
Television became my distraction.

When I took Delaney out and saw the night sky,
the connection with you returned immediately.
It happened so quickly, but I remember
the simultaneous gasp of beauty and gratitude.

"Do not cling to me"
were the hardest words from my first retreat.
I felt them as a rebuke, but I was left
to struggle with the verse some more.

When I understood that He had to go to the Father
so that He could be *our* Father,
I understood the words were said gently, and Mary understood.
Christ had not and never has stopped His loving of us.

In that I trust. In You I trust.

—

Prodigal Son's Father

It seems that no matter where my prayer begins,
it usually ends up with the prodigal son's father.
Contemplating the prodigal son's father
has changed my life.

The prodigal son returned home with no trust and faith.
He had given up his son-ship for living the wild life.
He was seduced by the evil one into thinking
he would be happier partying away from home.

The story gives us more questions than answers.
How long did it take to forgive himself?
Did he believe he was living a dream and would someday wake up?
It's taken me most of my life to trust I am a beloved daughter.

I am guessing once the son could trust he was still beloved son,
he lived in a state of virtual gratitude,
a stance that the older brother did not know.
Could he move from feeling a martyr to beloved son as well?

The prodigal son's father was truly a selfless man.
Watching him looking out for his lost son,
one sees no self-pity, only the pain of lost love and hope.
It was hope that sent him to the hilltop.

A man who is filled with unconditional love, selflessness, and hope
will not be denied. As great the sin was of the sons,
they had experienced the love of this man raising them.
Somewhere inside of them were the fruits of such love.

The hope contained in this parable is the hope
Jesus has granted to me now.
The secret of the parables is they leave you changed.
This one has truly changed me inside out.

—

Retreat Journals

The retreat journals are different from the daily ones,
although I believe what Rahner taught
about finding the blessings in the ordinariness of the everyday life.
The poems seem to fulfill that.

The retreat journals are from the times I am more fully immersed
in experiential encounters with God.
They are rich mines of treasure gems,
as all experiences are with our God who is gentle.

The Christ in these experiences is very gentle and tender.
He can be direct with his gentleness, and for that, I am grateful.
For whatever reason, I cannot hear voices sounding harshness.
You can correct me all day long if done gently.

I actually long to be corrected
so that I am connected to kingdom truth.
My truth can become very convoluted in isolation.
Isolation is a temptation that The Lord frees me from.

Retreats take place in sacred places and experiences.
There is guidance and direction to stay on the path of God's truth,
which is today very different from the world's truth.
I am aware of needing more affirmation than most, and I am sorry.

There have been too many years of following false guides
and getting lost on the way.
They're not wasted years for I learned my weaknesses
and the fact I could ignore the truth in my gut.

Rereading the journal this week brought me back to
very sacred times and experiences I should be living, not forgetting.
Forgetting was a survivor skill honed in youth.
It gets in the way as an adult.

I suspect my trust will grow.
I pray my trust will deepen.
Trust can't be taught;
I must live it every single day and situation.

Amen. Alleluia.

—

School Child

St. Ignatius refers to God taking him as a schoolchild
to teach him about God and his creation.
It feels the same for me.
It's astounding how God has acted like a
private tutor in my faith life.

It has made me realize to what extremes God will go
(think the prodigal son's father and the good Samaritan)
to aid us in understanding the kingdom,
which is His love for us and ours for others.

He is always telling me to pay attention
and then calling me into experiences so I am able to believe.
Others don't seem to need the extra attention to follow Him.
I need to be knocked to the ground to have faith.

I think of how we would define "special education"
to parents and students:
"You learn differently so we must teach you differently."
I'm just grateful God has a special education program.

I have to stay with this concept so I don't fall into comparison
of not having as much faith as others.
We would also define "fair" as not everyone getting the same,
but everyone getting what they need.

Perhaps the older brother would have understood
why his father treated his brother in the way he did
if he truly understood just how fair God is.
God makes sure each of us are given what we need.

My trust system could not develop normally
and causes many spiritual stumbling blocks.
We all have different blind spots,
and I believe God's grace is there to meet all our needs.

He is even kind enough to give me the warning:
"Pay attention."

Trust: God's Diadem

Trust.
Perhaps the most precious of all the jewels in God's diadem.
For it is truly rare in its purest form.
Its delicateness and fragileness composing its very radiance.

Unlike a diamond, the strongest of all jewels,
which owes its beauty to the pressure through which it is formed.
Or gold, becoming more valuable through its testing by fire.
Trust is a jewel that can be broken and shattered.

Jewels are such precious gifts that we insure, secure,
and safeguard them through all means possible.
Trust.
A most precious gift to receive and give.
Do we afford it the same protection and security?
Do we know what it costs the one who gives?

Respect, love, and faith are given away,
not without some trepidation, a sense of risk.
But when I give you my trust,
I entrust to your keeping the most fragile,
the most delicate center of the heart
that is all of me.

For some, the giving comes naturally.
A cycle of trust born from a circle of love.
A circle of care that breathed life into them,
nurturing from birth their body, heart, and soul.

For others, it is a giving shrouded in an agony of fear.
Life did not nurture trust in us.
Yet we know. In some mysterious way we know…
It is only in the giving that we can enter into that circle of life.
A circle of trust born not from a circle of care and love,
but from desperate hope and sheer faith.

We are never too broken, too shattered
to have love breathe life into us, to be mended and healed.
Our hearts can still be nurtured.
Our souls radiate as they begin to pulsate, ever so gently,
becoming alive through the giving and the receiving
of perhaps the most precious of intimacy's deep gifts,
the surrender of sacred trust from one soul to another.

Trusting Denise

God has trusted me to survive
a childhood of sexual abuse.
Three dollops of grace and resilience he must have added.
Never once did he doubt me.

He trusted me with a good education,
a vocation with his children.
I made it my mission they would know their own strengths.
He trusted me to raise three children.

He trusted me to survive a divorce,
to beat poverty and food stamps in a system
fraught with prejudices against stay-at-home moms.
The field we call education.

He trusted me with his children as a counselor.
To put a molester in jail,
to teach parents how to parent,
and teachers to have compassion.

He trusted me to survive the death of my first born,
and believe in the resilience of the twins.
Mentors stepped in, I could not be mother *and* father.
Fr. Ken taught me about young men, God, and ministry.

He trusted me to be persecuted for being compassionate,
again, I could never have done it alone.
He trusts me with ministry,
to bring others to Christ.

He trusts me to write.
To express our relationship in words that aren't enough.
He always knows when it's the best I can do.

He trusts me with retirement—to become who he made me to be.
To serve where he wants me to serve,
To grandparent the magnificent seven,
and to move more reflectively through the remainder of my years.

—

Trusting in Us

Do we ever stop and wonder about
how much God trusts us?
Since He is love
He is also a vulnerable God.

He trusts us to raise newborn babies;
we are temporary guardians.
He trusts us with the care of His creation.
His world—we must respect all since it is to be shared.

We all know the power of having someone believe in us.
He trusts us to believe in Him—
not only believe in Him but believe in His works,
His love for us.

We all know what it is like to be rejected.
Jesus was rejected by his own people.
Yet He never stopped believing in His Father.
He showed us His Father as the prodigal son's father.

Many of us didn't understand the concept of "father"
until He came to give us His.
"I am going to my Father and your Father,"
he told Mary Magdalene.

Since God is humble enough to give us free will,
it is our choice to believe in Him or not.
Where do you stand? What are you going to do?
Follow Him and build his kingdom?

He knows we cannot do it on our own,
so He created grace and made it a pure gift.
None of us are worthy—don't even go there.
Simply accept Him with your heart wide open.

The deepest act of humility we are asked to do or be,
day in and day out, over and over again.
Do you believe in Him as He believes in you?
It is much to ponder.

—

Waiting in the Nothing

There are times in the waiting when nothing
is happening.
The anticipation isn't even present
to make the time bearable.

Nothing.
Time feels like it has stopped
dead in its tracks.
Nothing.

It's hard to believe something is happening in the nothing.
It takes pure faith that God is working
in us and for us without our feeling anything.
Boredom is the greatest temptation.

No, doubt is the greatest temptation.
The temptation is to think you have been abandoned,
when in fact Christ is growing in us.
We do ridiculous things to pass the time.

Christ wants us to trust and not distract ourselves.
Something hard to do.
Trusting and believing are perhaps the hardest He asks us to do.
I imagine Jesus and the Father discussed this in prayer.

He actually tells us—it is not a secret conversation—
"Father, your will be done, not mine."
The courage it takes to say such words...
He sweats blood.

My dreams seem to try and make up for this time.
In my dreams, I am on exciting vacations
and hate to wake up to the nothing again.
I have to make a statement of faith.

Each and every morning.   —

Abandonment of Faith

Abandonment in work
is not an act of pure faith.
There is the return of accomplishment.
For some a sacrifice of time and self
for some the reward of losing touch with that self.

Abandonment into a lover's arms
is but a small leap of trust,
for he or she is physically there with us
to hold in great comfort and tenderness.
We may be betrayed or rejected.
It is not without risk.

Abandonment into parenting,
we place our own vulnerability
into the hands of dependent, helpless children.
No guarantees, no sure rewards.
but a choice we made and follow through unconditionally loving.
Knowing, yet not always realizing its impact,
the pure gift of parenting is when we let go.

Daily we abandon ourselves.
Sometimes work, love for others,
maybe just a good book that captures us.
We see it. We are aware. We know the cost.

Abandonment into our God.
Is it no different than work, child, lover?
Why does it seem like a trust beyond all other trusts?
Maybe because He is God,
and being God, he believes in us more than children, work, lovers.
Like any worthy parent or mentor,
he will call us beyond what we know
because he is beyond what we know.

So we must trust beyond what we can see
with an abandonment that is pure,
with a faith we are continually surprised by.
It can be light
It gets very dark.
It is very silent.
Its roar wakes the dead from their sleep.

But he calls me.
He loves me into this.
He leads me into this,
sometimes leaving me alone into this.

All I know is when called by name, I go.

Shadow Light

Bringing light and dark together
does not diminish the light,
as white mixed with black makes gray.
The light transforms the dark.

The dark is what is hidden out of sight,
covered up or is it under?
The danger stalks when we do not know and cannot see.
Why do we always tremble before the unknown?

As the monsters in our nights
become tamed in the light of the day,
we really have to admit we recognize
the shadows once they are brought to light.

Like intruding, unwelcome guests,
they will not be turned away.
Demanding entry into our lives,
how quickly they make a mess
of what we once thought was "our identity."

The truth is, we really are messy creatures,
imperfect, impetuous, falling down over and again.
"For I do not do what I want, but do what I hate" (Rom. 7:15).

We continue to throw our spiritual temper tantrums,
still under the delusion we can make the difference.

But, Abba,
loving us always in our totality
can do what we are powerless to do (Rom. 8:3).
In the tenderness of his encompassing embrace,
He heals our wounds of perfectionism,
redeeming our shadow light.

CHAPTER VIII

Love

Children of God

Words we hear, read, and say
all the time,
so we become immune to the meaning.
The reality goes beyond our understanding.

We are a child of God!
Since he is God, he loves us beyond
the love we have for our children and grandchildren.
That's unfathomable, so we take it on faith.

Probably every woman pregnant
with her second child worries if she can possibly
love a new child as much as her present child.
When the child comes, we enter into the life and love of God.

The nature of love is that it expands.
The more we love, the more we have to give.
No, it doesn't make sense…
The kingdom doesn't make sense.

But it makes all the sense in the world
once you have experienced it.
Once experienced,
it is life-changing.

The world of the kingdom
is more real than the world we live in now.
Sometimes it can be disorienting,
until we begin to actually live in it.

Children of God.
How can we take the most miraculous
meaning of our lives for granted?
Living in the wonder of it all makes our lives a liturgy.

Cycle of Growth

By journaling I find how growth is cyclical.
It's sometimes embarrassing how much so.
One day I threw away my just completed journal.
The last page read just like the first page!

In class I explain it by saying
it is like studying American history.
We study it in third grade, eighth, high school, and college.
We go deeper and are more mature.

Is this true of our weaknesses?
God has to start simple and then work
His way down deep,
until we are mature enough to understand?

I suspect that maturity will come on our deathbed.
Forgive me if there is a scent of hopelessness.
It is really just the opposite;
God will give us all the chances and time we need.

There is so much freedom and relief in this!
Where else do we get freedom and all the time we need?
Only someone so completely in love with us
could afford to be this generous.

—

Living in the Palm of Your Hand

Feeling your loving gaze as you hold me.
Realizing the protection as you shelter me.
Living the intimacy between us.
Safety in the security of your protection.

Being childlike, not childish.
Trusting crushes doubts.
Believing deepens faith.
Being held comforts wounds.

Gratitude focuses adoration.
Adoration gives purpose for being.
Being fulfills your desires for me.
Hope propels me forward.

Night is lived in the light.
The light is eternity,
You hold the world in the palm
of your hand.

You are that big.
You are that loving.
You are forgiving and merciful.
Your people are truly blessed.

"For You are our God, and we are your people."
We live this daily
and take it seriously.
We are your covenant people, and we praise you.
Amen.

—

"Maybe I Could Have Loved You..."

I heard this song on the television
and sobbed all night.
I had never heard it before
and it touched a deep spot inside.

It took me to the core of my vulnerability,
a topic my director and I have been back and forth on this Advent,
so my reaction didn't really come out of nowhere,
but the intensity blindsided me.

Suddenly my love for everyone in my life wasn't enough.
The tears for not loving God enough were the deepest,
yet I knew there is no way
He can be loved enough except by the God in us.

Maybe that is where the tears were coming from,
The center where God lives in me,
but I am always aware to be enough;
must come from him.

Knowing that makes me aware of the roadblocks
and other distractions that I carefully construct
to fight what I most long for.
Why do I do that? Why can't I stop it?

This is the core of where the tears were originating—
I can't do it, yet I block him at times.
It makes absolutely no sense at all, and I don't understand
it other than not "loving Him more than I could have."

The deepest tabernacle within me where God resides
has a sacristan that sometimes wanders away
and neglects her role in keeping the fire burning.
Like the virgins awaiting the bridegroom.

—

Mutual Love

Love that is not returned is extremely painful
and leaves a person filled with doubt of self-worth.
There have been experiences of God returning my love
(remembering it is He who loves first).

My retreats have been the most powerful of this mutual love.
Sadly, there have been many more times of
evil convincing me of rejection and being unlovable.
My past often sneaks itself into my present.

Throughout my life, God has gifted me with gifts of Himself
that could not be argued, doubted, or disbelieved.
But in my weakness of unworthiness, I would forget them.
The writings he has been sending seem to be
more like engravings than writings.

Another term for the "wounds of love"
could be called "engravings of love."
They are permanently etched into my heart and soul.
My hope is this is a permanent change.

How can words possibly describe being loved by Christ?
Our language does not contain the correct words to say it.
The best we can do, I have been doing for years.
"It feels like…"

Tonight I am not even going to try to write the feelings,
sensations, and reality. It is reality.
I know it is reality, but that is all I can write about it.
God's love cannot be contained in our small words.

I will just say thank you for all you have given me.
This journey, this guide who provides security and assurances.
This openness of my being
and the courage to accept You as my all.

—

My Father and I

"My Father and I will come and dwell in you."
The intimacy in this line is enough
to take my breath away.
Who could want any more than this?

For whatever reason, the word "dwell" connotes
a deeper reality than the word "live."
I'm not sure why.
Anyone can live anywhere, but to dwell suggests choice.

I think of Mary and the baby Jesus dwelling
in the purity of her womb.
We are made pure by living the commandments.
Pure enough that Jesus and the Father will dwell in us.

What was it like for Mary to know that Jesus
was dwelling and growing inside her womb?
What is it like for us to know Jesus
is dwelling and growing us into Him?

The Father calls all people to Himself
through Jesus, as Jesus told us.
Jesus is the Way, the Truth, and the Light.
Dwelling in us, he transforms us.

It is a gift that I cannot take for granted.
Conscious of the dwelling,
I long for the transformation that is taking place.
It means that I must listen, obey, and be pliable.

—

Night Presence

More often than not,
when the lights go out,
the awareness of God's presence
is made known.

The dark erases the images of things in my room.
The television is off, and books are put down.
There are no distractions
to keep me from His presence.

God's presence in the silent darkness is always a comfort.
He is gentle and wants nothing but to "be with."
There is no greater love than
two who just want to be "with each other."

When no one wants, demands, or asks anything of you,
there is a sacred presence to each other.
Each person is loved for who they are,
not what they can do for one another.

It is the relationship of love
in its highest and most pure form.
God's love is always in the purest form
for there is nothing the Creator needs from His creature.

Yet He created us because He wants our love,
our companionship with Him.
The silence of just being with Him
without asking for any signs —wanting just Him.

This is the silent, night presence of Jesus.

—

Silent Lover

Present in your silence,
you enfold me tenderly in your love.
Your touch satisfies beyond any other.

Present in your absence,
I know yearning that speaks so deep,
only your love can
calm the storms of the searching.
A gift—albeit double-edged in its piercing.

Presence in absence,
your love is spoken in the silence of knowing
beyond all other forms of knowing.

Why is it this way with us?
Presence in the middle of absences?
Temptations hidden in loneliness?

Why?
Do you desire or do you challenge my quiet ways?
Yet I have found that words seem to dispel,
while silence instead intensifies.

Even these words are empty in themselves
and only speak in between the lines of experience,

Do you, have you, are you
claiming me as your own?
How am I to know?
And yet...has it ever not been so?

Were you not always there,
protecting, fathering, loving?
How often I abandoned you
when you came closest to
the very core of my vulnerability.

Presence in absence you are the silent lover
of my days and of my nights.
Were you not always there?
Has it ever not been so?

The Father's Mantle

One of the lines in the prodigal son parable
that strikes me to the core
is when the Father wraps his precious mantle
around his more precious son.

The act is one of deep reverence—maybe even liturgical.
His lost son was starved, shivering with
cold and fear, naked, and filthy.
All the father wanted was to surround his son
in his mantle of warmth, love, and symbolism.

I was chosen at baptism and given a white garment.
A clean, young, and innocent baby.
But now how I long to feel being wrapped
in Abba's mantle of forgiveness and love.

Is your mantle the necessary wedding clothes I need
to be allowed into the wedding feast?

Gathered in your own rich cloak
marks me as your chosen and beloved.

I yearn to feel it envelop me as I sleep,
knowing it is finally safe to rest in you.
Knowing I will wake up into your life,
wrapped securely in your care and protection.

Like the prodigal, I am stunned due to my unworthiness
but exploding with the joy of your response.
This is a miracle moment.
Even the sibling cannot understand and accept.

My longing is stronger than fighting the unworthiness.
It takes great humility to swallow pride
and accept the love of my Creator.
I am fully aware I am a creature elevated into him.

—

The Peace His Love Gives

There is nothing any of us desires more
than the peace His love gives.
It is different from the peace the world gives,
for that peace is temporary and not as deep.

The peace His love gives changes us immensely.
It is in the little things,
the pace we walk, eat, drive, and process.
His peace changes us in the big things as well.

The way we are not affected by every little change
in the landscape of our days.
We learn to roll with some of the changes,
knowing that we never were in charge in the first place.

Grace is another word for His peace.
Grace is what activates the peace that allows us
to function as His beloved.
We can feel the grace pour as we feel the rain come down.

It's all very simple if we pay attention.
To pay attention and feel it, we must be still
and know that He is God.
He finds us when we look for Him.

We don't find Him. He always finds us.
Even the searching for Him is His initiative.
We read a book that He chose, not us.
We go on retreat only to find He brought us there.

All He needs for his loving and caring for us
is our yes.
As Mary's yes was a continuous daily prayer,
so our yes is our daily prayer.

—

Who Are You?

How come my love for you is so consuming?

My desire for you is all based on your desire for me.
Do you know how crazy that sounds?
You are the Creator of the universe,
and I am a grain of sand on the beach.

It is so astounding sometimes I am tempted to walk away—
this is too preposterous to be true!
Sometimes I have run away,
but you have such a hold on me I keep coming back.

How does a grain of sand talk about God?
How does she even think she can find the words?
Even that makes it hard to believe
You defy reason and logic.

Thank you for loving me beyond logic and reason.
If you hadn't, I would just be another agnostic,
instead of an "in love" follower.
Being in love with you makes no sense.

I can't call you on the phone, text, or email.
We can't meet for dinner, although you do feed us.
How do I find out how you are doing, what's on your mind?
When asked where you stay, you simply answered, "Come and see."

Maybe that is the answer to all my questions.
The answers are only found in following you to see.
It's not like you don't want us—
You invite us over and over again.

For you to answer me in words would teach me nothing.
At least not at the level you want me to learn.
There is only one way to can tell us who you are.
"Come and see…"

—

Who Is This Man Who Teaches and Listens?

During His public ministry, Jesus
exemplified compassion, listening, and teaching.
Any teacher will tell you they have to teach.
It's a part of a teacher's DNA.

What Jesus learned from the Father
He had to turn and teach us.
This is true of any teacher—
whatever we learn we want to teach.

There is a difference between a teacher
and someone who gives lectures.
A teacher has to listen to the students
in order to know how to teach.

A teacher who cannot listen
is a teacher who cannot teach.
That is how we know Jesus is always listening to us.
He came to teach us the Way.

He wants to know what we hear,
how we heard it, and how we feel about it.
He wants to know how we process
and only we can tell Him.

A true parent listens to each of their children.
They are all different.
It is the only way they know what and how to teach them.
They grow and learn in their individual ways.

Jesus created us—He knows we are each unique.
There are no words to express the depth of joy,
knowing He is listening
to all that is happening in our hearts and souls.

CHAPTER IX

Scripture

Follow Me

"Come and follow me,"
Jesus continuously invites and calls.
When I ask Him, "Where?"
the penetrating return gaze
exacts trust and faith from within.

"Are we almost there?"
the child in me pesters.
"Not likely,"
His silence responds.

"I'm hungry and thirsty!"
the child in me starts to complain.
Sometimes I am fed and temporarily satisfied.
If not, I struggle to feed upon faith.
He is satisfied.

"Are we ever going to stop?"
I look around and find the answer
from and within my fellow companions.
"Once you choose this path,
we sometimes rest, but we do not stop."
I hear Him give a patient sigh.

"I can't see anything."
This never works the way the child wants.
So I draw upon Fr. Ken's advice:
"Learn to see with the eyes of the soul."
And I feel God smile,
as any parent would.

"I want to go back home!"
I wearily yet defiantly demand.
His gentle response pulls the defiance from the fear,
and quietly He responds,
"That is exactly where we are going."

The child now silenced with loving admonition,
begins again to follow in quiet surrender.

Living Scripture

The most profound experience of Scripture
is that it is a living document.
Each time we read and enter a passage
we are at a different point in our journey.

Therefore the Spirit is always teaching us through the Word.
but it is up to us the pick it up; read, study,
and enter into its passages.
To name a few, I have been the woman with the alabaster jar,
a servant girl at Cana and at the Last
Supper, and a babysitter for Jesus.

The insights and experiences with the Living Word
move us from one place to another
in our spiritual journey
and our relationship with Christ.

It is like the parables—
we cannot hear a parable and remain unchanged.
We have to make a decision to move into the kingdom
or to walk away from the parable and its message.

In periods of dryness, I must admit
reading Scripture is like eating straw.
The dryness within me has removed all taste
and life from Scripture.

We learned from Ignatius
that God allows these periods of desolation for His reasons—
reasons that we must look at to see where we fall
and act on it or wait it out.

In prayer we surrender,
and we wait…and wait.
The waiting I believe itself is an act of faith and prayer.
We acknowledge God is God, and we are his creatures.

Consolation will eventually follow desolation.
This Ignatius believed in so strongly,
he charges us to prepare for desolation when in consolation.
Not so easy because part of consolation is feeling it will last forever.

This is why we put our trust in the genius of Ignatius.

—

Mary Magdalene

I believe Mary a role model for all women
in love with Jesus, divine, and human.
She owed him much because he healed her of her demons.
We love Him for His healing of us.

As women we may experience being on the margins of society
as she was. It still happens.
Many of us have been sinned against,
and sometimes the victim is treated as the sinner.

Being healed, dignified, restored, and respected is the
greatest gift given to marginalized women.
We learn that we can love and be loved in return
we become whom God created us to be.

We are daughters, mothers, wives, single women, and lovers.
We all have our roles to live out.
No matter the role—the love is intense.
we need His love to be who we are.

We follow him as did Mary.
How could we not remain with Him?
Care for Him, listen to Him, and learn from Him,
He who made us whole.

Mary,
We thank you for your courage, your love, your example.
We thank you for going to the disciples
and announcing your truth:
"I have seen the Lord."

"I too have seen the Lord."
Amen.

"My Lord and My God!"

Words that speak the adoration within.
Words, yet they maintain the silence.
Union. Communion. Recognition.
He is my God, and I am his beloved.

Words uttered in Scripture
words from an astonished doubter.
The most repeated prayer I pray.
"My Lord and my God!"

How many words are there in Scripture?
How many books written of our God?
Do we really need anymore?
Don't these words say all that can be said?

"My Lord and my God!"
If I say no more,
all will have been said.

Road to Emmaus

While out on the nature trail,
it was easy to imagine the two disciples
walking home in keen disappointment.
They had believed in Jesus, and he was killed.

We each have a story of someone who has let us down.
Maybe it was a promise broken.
Maybe they did not live up to whom
they proclaimed to be to us.

The danger in many of these incidents
is we let our expectations get the better of us.
Like the two disciples, we project our expectations
onto the situation, therefore distorting reality.

Jesus had to remind them of the Scripture predictions
that they had forgotten.
They wanted a Messiah to release them from the Romans,
not realizing the true Messiah released them from death.

Do I look for the immediate reward,
forgetting that God is able to see the bigger picture?
Do I trust in the Lord enough to know
He has my best interests at heart?

They "recognized Him in the breaking of the bread."
Do I recognize Him in the same way?
Sometimes I am the bread that needs to be broken
before I recognize it is my false expectations
that need to be broken before I can receive Him.

"Did not our hearts burn within us?"
This is one of my favorite lines from Scripture
because when Christ reveals Himself,
my heart does burn within me.

There is no greater joy than having the Lord
come and stay with me.
As He did with the disciples,
He uses the Scriptures to point out what I have forgotten.

The Greatest Love Story Ever Told

Of course I am referring to Scripture.
There are probably as many definitions of Scripture
as there are people.
It is not only a work of love but a literary phenomenon.

Scholars and ordinary people alike read
scripture from many different perspectives.
It is never the same story for we are never the same person.
The OT used to scare me until I understood covenant.

That is when I first saw it as a love story.
It was alive only in my intellect.
As the internship and exercises internalized,
the stories of Jesus became love stories of the heart.

During the recent terror attacks and natural disasters,
I never blamed God.
He is too much of an active lover in life.
The stories of His life have become my stories.

Perhaps that needs some clarification so others
will not take that as an aggrandizement statement.
It means that I have fallen in love with Him
and am therefore in love with His teachings—how he lived.

When you love someone, you naturally want to emulate them.
They say couples start to look and act alike after years of marriage.
The same is true after loving Christ so long.
I pray that it is "no longer I who live, but He who lives in me."

There can be no higher calling and purpose to life—
to live so that it is Christ living in me.
This is what I mean by "being prayer."
My life becomes prayer in the ordinary days of living.

As we spoke of in the peer group,
this is not an intellectual process.
It's about the feelings of the heart now.
Or as our pastor often said, "It's all about relationship."

It's about the relationship with Christ,
but as John spoke with so much clarity—
also the relationship with our brothers and sisters.

To Be So Loved

I can now put myself into the place of the wounded traveler,
picked up and taken to an inn for healing and safety.
For the first days, he must have been disoriented,
wondering where he was and how he got there.

The innkeeper's story must have sounded like a dream
that he was afraid to wake up and find wasn't true.
As his injuries healed and his mind became clear,
his gratitude must have overwhelmed him.

After being robbed by some of the worst of humanity,
he was saved by the best of our humanity.
He must have known that the Samaritan
had divinity in his heart.

It is a disarming reality to find oneself so loved.
There are no words, no forms of gratitude
to express such a sacred feeling.
Is there no greater feeling than to know you are loved?

Not just loved in a general sense of how we use the term
but loved to the point of being taken care of
and having our needs met, needs we might not even be aware of.
God knows us through and through and knows what we don't.

No one likes self-pity, but compassion is real and necessary.
Even when David died, there was a part of me that fought
people feeling sorry for me. I don't know what that is.
All I wanted was their companionship and understanding.

It is the same with the abuse.
The triggers and flashbacks are very embarrassing,
and I am only comfortable telling the details to one person.
If others ask, I speak in generalities.

Love takes us where we are, can see beyond where we are,
and receives us in our totality,
No matter the shame, goodness, or circumstances.
We are seen for who we are, not what was done to us.

Love is seeing the whole person as a beloved child of God,
until we are so loved we can see ourselves as the same.
There is no greater gift of love.

All That I Am

Weep, my child,
for all that you must weep.
Ache, my child,
for all that you must ache.
Yearn, my child,
for all that burns within.

So much that could have been
wasn't.
So much you never dared dream of
is.

Under your tears,
behind the doors yet to be opened,
there is love and purity
yet to be experienced,
still to be grown into.
In time that you do not understand,
in joys and pain you do not comprehend,
in ways that are not your ways,
but My way for you.

Listen for sounds yet to be heard.
See with a vision yet to be focused.
Learn with wisdom beyond earthly knowledge.
Touch with a gentleness beyond your gentle soul.
Love with a love beyond what your heart can know.

Weep, my child,
for all that you weep.
Sleep now all you must sleep
so that you will awake
to all that I AM.

More Song of Songs

"I sleep, but my heart is awake.
I hear my love knocking."
In the stillness of my sleep,
the waves of the spirit praise through me,
rocking me gently through the night.

"Open to me, my beloved."
So frightening to try, so much courage…
And it was a love like no other love affair.
No words in prayer,
journal pages left barren.
Silence.
Deep silence echoing love so pure.

"I opened to my love,
but he has turned and gone.
My soul fails at his flight."
Abandoned? Rejected?
Left to search and not find?
Can I do this again?

It is different this time
for there is difference between
what was despair and hopelessness,
and being "sick with love."

"What makes your love better than other lovers?"
"Is he not like all others fickle in fancy, fast in flight?"

No.
What makes my love better than other lovers
"is that my love is mine, and I am his."
Beyond these comings and goings
beyond the now sleepless nights,
the searching and the longing…

There is one thing I know that I did not know before
that teaches me to trust and surrender.
"My love is mine, and I am his."

Part of the Journey Home

The torn and weary lamb limps on home
after days and nights skirmishing among wolves.
He told her it would be like this,
even though victory was already won.

The wolves ripped into her faith,
gnashing their sharp teeth into doubts,
exposing weaknesses and sins.
She is humbled to the ground.

They hate where she is heading,
and to Whom this sheep belongs.

The inner battles moved to the outside
where the demons were more defined,
flashbacks leaving her disoriented.

She only longs to find her Shepherd,
who watched from a distance ready to act,
but preferring she learn to endure,

She only longs to find her Shepherd,
to lean her wounded body in comfort to his.
Hoping for shelter, healing, and rest,
until He sends her out again, lamb among the wolves.

She doesn't ask "Why?" anymore,
trusting in her Shepherd and the director
he sent who guides her through these times.
Knowing in the midst of the pain,
victory is already won.

Suffering and Prayer

Some spiritual writers have written about
how suffering and prayer
transforms us from self focus
into caring for others.

"Without a hurt, the heart is hollow,"
Josh Groban sings on his CD.
Anyone who picks up a newspaper can see suffering happens.
Without prayer to guide us, we could turn cynical and pessimistic.

With prayer, we can learn that we are not alone in our suffering.
Jesus promised that He would always be with us.
Any crisis tugs at our heartstrings,
and there is an outpouring of help and empathy.

Empathy is lacking in the person of no prayer.
Their ego is their center, and there is only room for self.
Will their power, pride, and possessions
give them the purpose for their being?

Can there be any meaning in life,
when life is centered on no one but self?
How can life have any meaning
without being connected to something greater than ourselves?

I think the key word in all of this is connection.
To live in the kingdom now, we must be connected.
Connected to God, we know our true self
and our relation to Him and all others.

That connection keeps us grounded in reality,
Not an alternative reality we create ourselves.
That only leads to thinking we are the center,
while prayer teaches the center is found through compassion.

Jesus was the essence of compassion.
Prayer teaches us how to be compassionate
as He was compassionate.
As we are to be compassion.

Suffering

When reflecting on my life it is the joys
I automatically focus on.
This is the gift of children and grandchildren.
But the spiritual writers talk about the importance of suffering.

So I take off the denial blinders to look at the pain.
There has been plenty, as probably true
for all of us.
It has played an important role in our identity.

Like all our experiences,
it has formed us into who we are today.
When the twins lost their older brother,
resiliency, maturity and wisdom grew in both of them.

Paying attention to the inner movements
inside of us helps us to grow
into the wise and understanding people
God wants all of us to be.

There is less paying attention to self
and looking through the eyes of others.

Suffering leads to dependence upon God,
and what follows then is the awareness
that God is all that matters.
Self-importance, but not identity, is lost in divine union.

Living in God brings such joy that I am content.
As long as I am in Him,
my importance matters not.

Today

All I have is now.
It's all any of us have.
Yet I worry, wish, and hope,
this is not being in the now.

It's a natural thing to do,
except God is supernatural.
I have studied and worked and prayed
and still forget this truth.

"It is what it is."
A phrase now so popular it is trivialized.
Is it not saying the same thing?
All I have is the now and its acceptance.

It is a radical shift for someone like me.
Having to heal the past
automatically makes me look to the future.
Retirement looks endless when looking at years instead of a day.

The day.
It's all I have and no more.
David's last an October 15th.
So this should be engraved in my heart.

It is.
When I remember. Help me, Lord.
Memory.
Gift, not burden.

Hope in the Desert

"I am your primary relationship. Center in me."
In abandonment and abuse, you were there.
But, Jesus, I did not know it.
How can love exist
in the midst of evil violence?
I feared you above all others.

"I am your primary relationship. Center in me."
In loss, pain, loneliness, you are here.
How can your divine presence
exist in the middle of hopelessness?
I seek you above all others.

You are the silence in the empty echoes
of the screaming taking place within.
You are the trembling that is
surfacing and releasing the memories.
You are the tears
in the pain of despair.
I find you in all others.

Faith. Trust. Hope.
Overused in my education,
underdeveloped in life.
Until now when there is nothing else.

Only faith, trust, and hope.
When flashbacks catapult me back in time.
When forgotten past shame
crashes into present consciousness,
leaving me stunned, dazed, confused.

Faith.
Believing you are present
in shame and fear.

Trust.
Believing you are good over evil.
Presence in abandonment.

Hope.
Believing you are love
in the midst of loss.
Believing you are the one
who holds and brings all life together
in the middle of the desert.

CHAPTER X

Abuse and Spirituality

A Grief Wound

Deep inside there is a wound, a hole
that is inflamed and bleeding.
In it is the absence of all those I am grieving.
One grief begets another and another.

"Name it," my director has always told me.
There is the father hole, the lack of trust.
My mother, David, and Delaney.

There are times it throbs like it did last Saturday,
raging over the abuse and lack of trust and protection.

It is something that is inconceivable,
so it makes no sense attempting to understand
what can never be understood.
The rage is not just for me, but all of us betrayed.

Wound connects to wound to wound.
We are all in this together.
We faced it alone then;
it's not right to face it alone now.

There needs to be someone safe now in our lives
whom we can reach out to and let them know
something new has surfaced.
It's crucial to know that someone else knows.

It is enough to know I am not alone
in rage, grief, abandonment, and rejection.
It may have taken place years and years ago,
but each new memory makes it raw.

The rawness brings out the intense vulnerability again.
It may be years, but if the discovery is now,
the pain and shame are now.
Not something to face alone.

We do not have to.
Jesus told us He was going to the Father
to make His Father, Our Father.
In this we can trust and take comfort.

Forgiveness for My Father

When forgiveness comes after twenty-some years,
it is not to be taken lightly.
There were earlier times of forgiveness that did not hold.
Forgiveness in Loyola was different because "I got my dad back."

That was how I knew it was true forgiveness.
It was no accident it happened at Loyola.
The only way there was room inside to receive my father back
was if the forgiveness released what was blocking me.

Once I was angry with a person close to me,
and at mass that afternoon, the priest said,
"If you are too angry to forgive, it is okay
because God has forgiven for you."

He went on to say the last thing a person needed to hear
is that they must forgive.
After that homily, I was never angry at that person again.

Forgiveness for my father was not something I could do
on my own. It was a gift from the Spirit
on a pilgrimage to Spain.

"Jesus Touched Them"

Right after the Transfiguration,
the apostles lay prostrate in fear.
Jesus went to reassure them but knew to touch them
while saying "Do not be afraid."

Why do we ever doubt that Jesus knows
what we are going through?
Without his touch,
His words might have been interpreted as judgmental.

Touch.
Appropriate, loving, and gentle touch.
Unites, comforts, and nurtures us.
One person filled with compassion for another.

One of the physical aftermaths of abuse
is the startle effect—leaving us to jump if a loud noise
or unexpected touch happens.

Yet in reality, safe touch is one of the most healing
of all the cures that are out there.
The startle effect comes and goes
until it is only present in experiencing a flashback.

"Jesus touched them."
Jesus touches people quite often throughout the gospels.
He created us.
He knows our basic human needs.

Layers of Emptying

After giving away nine bags of books,
I'm at it again.
I went through the shelves and found more books,
more furniture, clothes, and stuff.

God empties me in layers.
It is the only way I could survive

Even though I can write about spiritual emptying,
I'm perfectly well aware of how tightly my hands are clenched
and holding onto characteristics that get in His way.
I know it from the pain.

During abuse therapy, I was told it was necessary
to give up disassociating.
I looked at the therapist in disbelief
it took a long time to learn that skill.

Give it up? Why would that be a good thing?
He said although it was necessary to survive,
it was now getting in the way of being healthy.
Getting in the way…

Although I don't know all the things
getting in the way of my deeper relationship with God,
there are many. It has to be a lifelong process.
This is probably why we can't see God and live.

The cleansing and dark nights seem
to necessarily come in layers.
His way of eliminating what is getting in the way
of healthy and total oneness.

Protection

Words cannot describe the peace, security, and comfort
that comes from having protection.
Every child born needs and deserves protection,
but sadly that is not always the case.

For a child without protection,
it is okay if it comes later in life.
There is more gratitude for the gift,
and there is much healing.

The prodigal son's father protected both his sons.
He protected as best he could the prodigal's reputation,
perhaps at the cost of his own. He did not care.
He protected the elder son by telling him all he had was his.

To discover Abba as protector is to be given
a prodigal son's father to protect me.
He heals the shame.
He gives total unconditional love.

To have a human protector
means that I can trust my journey
will stay spiritually and psychologically healthy.
There is great trust in knowing this.

To have my son, who is in the kingdom
protecting our family and leading me to God,
is a gift of great security, hope, and peace.
He protects as any son would.

Yes, my protection came late in life.
But it does not matter now that it is present.
Abba, as any good father,
knows the needs of His children and provides.

Protector

Abba, Father,
Thank you for protecting me as a young child,
making sure the tabernacle inside was never violated.
It is why I can call you Abba.

The times between flashbacks are longer.
They decrease in number and occurrence.
But there other instances that I can only name
"shamebacks."

They are not memories or pictures surfacing.
It feels like a tender spot has been poked.
The only image that comes to me is someone
poking a stick into a hornet's nest.

What comes out are the feelings from the times
the pictures/memories took place.
I feel the need to apologize for being the way I am—
for having secrets that need to stay hidden.

There is a shame to being me that I can't scrub off
no matter how hard and often I try.
It used to be my entire existence,
thanks to Your grace it only surfaces once in a while.

It smells and sounds like evil.
To be able to discern that makes it a little easier.
Yet when it does happen, I need to seek your protection
so that it does not devour me.

It is like quicksand, and I need your saving hand.

Scars

It was one thing for Jesus to become one of us,
to empty himself to take the form of a slave,
obedient to be killed by crucifixion.
He rose again after three days.

What I have struggled with and at the same time
been in awe of is that the resurrection
did not erase his scars.
God has scars.

That seems so wrong for one who is pure,
one who is God.
Some people wear their scars like badges of honor.
Jesus was too humble for that.

If anyone doubts the humanity of Jesus,
reflecting on this may give them thought.
If Jesus was only divine and not human,
he would not have had scars in his resurrection.

Part of the human condition is we are scarred,
by something we did or was done to us.
As simple as falling off a bike
to the scars of being sinned against.

Why did Jesus still have scars?
He wanted to teach us his humanity was real.
He was like us in all things except sin.
Human beings are scarred.

Yes there is true healing, forgiveness, and moving forward.
We need not dwell on the past,
only recognize its part in forming who we are.

Beloved Daughter

When asked how I have changed inside,
the answer shot out without thinking:
"Beloved daughter."
It's been pondered ever since.

To come from a little girl who believed she was "dirty"
to beloved daughter
has been a lifelong journey.
My prodigal father was not to be denied.

Love, and only love, could heal the wounds of betrayal
the love and belief of teachers who believed in me
long before I could begin to believe in myself.
Their patience became my hope.

I remember the nightmares, hiding in closets,
forced into evil environments when innocent.
The prodigal son was living in the mud of swine,
as was I.

The Father knew what it would take to heal me
into becoming who he always saw me,
His beloved daughter
rather than the trash I believed I was.

When I look back at the miracle of my journey
and see His orchestrated twists and turns
the people he sent, the experiences of great grace
I realize He was creating me the whole time.

My creation has lasted almost seventy years so far.
It didn't begin and end on July 22nd
He has been creating and birthing me my entire life.
It's what Thomas Merton saw in downtown Louisville—

We are all shining lights. All miracles born of Love
all gift to ponder…

Into Your Hands

My spirit wearies from the battle,
but moves from "Your will be done"
to "Into your hands."
Not a discernible difference
for those filled with deep faith.
A step made possible
only through your daily call.

Sometimes raging, sometimes silent,
the battle now seems part of everyday life.
You call me day and night.
Each call a renewal of hope.
Energy moving toward you,

"Always return to your safe place,"
advice sustaining me through this.
You are there,
not caring that I don't understand,
not judging or rejecting the fury within.
Only loving, gently caring, earnestly nourishing.

It is my battle,
but you do not leave me totally alone.

Abandonment and surrender,
words of abuse, pain, and guilt
for the abused child.

Abandonment and surrender.
Prayer of love and trust
for the grown-up child.

In a world of confusion and contradiction,
where good and evil push and pull.
Into your hands
is the safest place of refuge.
Is this the sacred home of your promise? (John 14)

CHAPTER XI

Advent and Christmas

Praise to Mary

How do we thank you, Mary, for your yes?
Little did you know at the time what that yes would cost.
But also, little did you know the grace and blessings
you would receive not only for yourself, but for us.

What was it like the first time you felt Jesus in your womb?
Did the "affirmation of being overshadowed by the Sprit"
bring you to your knees in prayer and tears?
You knew it in your head, but now in your body and heart.

For certain, there were some who scoffed at you,
becoming pregnant without "knowing man."
I can imagine the gossip and scorn surrounding you,
when all you did, in total obedience and faith, was to answer "Yes."

You carried the Christ Child in your womb
for us.
You suffered the scandal of being an unwed mother
for us.
You taught Jesus everything a mother teaches
for us.

You suffered your child going against your established religion
for us.
You suffered the greatest of all pain at the foot of the cross
for us.

Growing up, I could not relate to you because you were put
on a pedestal so high, it was hopeless to even think of reaching you.
Then I became a mother.
While holding Jeff screaming in pain for twenty-
four hours, I prayed with you.

Suddenly I entered your life, and you entered mine.
Motherhood made us one with each other.
My first response all those years ago was "Thank you."
Forty-some years later, my thank you is deeper
than I could have ever imagined.

The only appropriate response now is to follow you,
learn from you, pray with you, be like you.
You are guiding us through this life
as you wait for us in the next.
Amen.

Advent Vulnerability

Advent invites us to once again realize with deep shock
that God took the form of a dependent baby within Mary.
It is a shock if we ponder it for more than ten seconds,
and it is beyond our limited human comprehension.

The incarnation makes no sense if you know not God.
If you know Him, he has gifted you with the why.
There is only one reason for the why—
it is love that knows no bounds.

Why would He do this for us?
Because He loves us.
Why would He become vulnerable for us?
Because He loves us.

As God, He chose to be humiliated, rejected, and killed.
Mary, his mother, said yes to the same
humiliation and vulnerability.
Vulnerability is something we humans flee from
at every possible juncture in our lives.

We are an Advent people when we ponder
the season and its ramifications.
What some deem to be insanity,
others take face on. Why?
Because of the love He came to give.

It is saying yes to the grace of His vulnerability.
It will leave scars in the aftermath of victory.
No one of us is left unscathed
when we say yes to Advent grace and become vulnerable.

And share in the victory!

Christmas Expectations

It is easy to let the world seduce us this time of year.
Make the perfect holiday—you are responsible for making the joy.
The commercials on TV are Currier and Ives fairy tales,
and none of us are very good at reconstructing fairy tales.

The amount of presents does not matter.
If it does to your children, you have some gratitude lessons to teach.
Greed, materialism, and entitlement are serious problems today.
Treating these problems are more our job than creating fairy tales.

Learn from the youngest children,
it's not the number of gifts,
it is the lights on the Christmas tree,
the family traditions repeated each year. They can be quite simple.

Lucy helps me wrap all the presents.
The other kids and I make a simple Christmas candy.
It's the joy of the snow if it becomes a white Christmas.
It is the company or guests whom we invite.

Little children are happy with the simple.
Christ told us to become like the children.
Are we too happy with the simple?
How much of Christmas is simply the anticipation?

The Advent wreath, trips to decorated churches,
and going up to the manger in wonder and awe.
If Christmas does not bring out the wonder and awe in you,
no matter what your age, you can make it happen this Christmas.

Become like the little children.

Christmas Love

Christmas faith…
Mary quietly showing us how to live
this mystery born of Christmastide.
Her pondering teaching us how
to travel the dry deserts of doubt with humility.

Joseph, model for all who want to follow their own way
until angels deliver God's other plans.

The magi, following only a star shining through darkness,
showing us how to follow this same star that calls us,
so that we may also worship and adore,
and present to this Child the gift of ourselves,
pledging our fidelity and loyalty to this newborn King.

"At the name of Jesus, every knee shall bend,"
as did Mary, Joseph, and the magi
following Christmas faith.

Stars, gifts, stable, and swaddling clothes
symbols for what is so beyond my words,
my ability to explain.

Christmas faith.
Having no plans but God's plans for us.
Journeying through dark valleys and hills
not sure of where we are going and if we will get there.

But continuing on with stumbling faith
saying our own yes so God may journey
to the center of our heart
where Christmas love is born.

The Vulnerability of Christmas

There is a certain vulnerability of Christmas
that carries over from our childhood.
Have we been good?
Will Santa come?

But it's stronger when we approach the manger,
looking at the Christ Child.
The vulnerability takes on a tenderness and wonder
that I always find bewildering.

It's good we celebrate it each year because
it takes a lifetime to ponder.
Do we ever fully take it in—
what our God has done for his people?

Each year my heart must stretch larger,
trying to find room to approach
the mystery of such a gift.
I cannot do it alone.

It takes at least twelve marked days of solemnity.
In reality it takes a lifetime.
Were there three kings?
They represent us.

To follow a star, on faith, into strange countries.
It is the search on which we all embark,
carrying the gift of self,
for that is all we have to give to God.

The spiritual world can be a strange country,
so we travel with others
seeking guidance on the way.
God always provides direction.

Twelve Days of Christmas

It surprises me that a culture so eager
to begin the Christmas season,
is not knowledgeable
of its true beginning and end.

There are twelve days of Christmas,
not twelve weeks that end on the 26th.
On the second day of Christmas,
the decorations come down, and the music stops.

Christmas stops just when it should be beginning.
It's sad to see trees dragged to the garbage pile.
Anthony cried last year when he found out the music stops
on the second day of Christmas.

Yesterday, fully emerged in the Spirit of the season
I turned on the radio expecting to hear the music.
But it starts before Halloween only to end the 26th.
Like Anthony, I was ready to cry.

For those who pray the liturgical season,
it makes it easy to understand and celebrate the twelve days.
The birth of "I AM"
takes time to contemplate and celebrate.

The awe cannot be turned off like the music
or taken down until next Halloween.
There is a grace in praying the season.
It keeps us grounded it the miracle.

The Alleluia Days

As I write of nothingness and waiting,
I'm somewhat aware the alleluia days are coming.
The liturgical and secular calendars say so.
We call it Christmas.

Only a few days after the winter solstice,
the blackness lifts long enough for joy to enter.
The love comes just in time to break the darkness.
We celebrate, love, and gift one another.

Some do it because the calendar says it is time.
It's Christmas again.
Some celebrate because they believe in Christ,
who gave us the only real reason to celebrate.

"Do this in memory of me."
Like the Eucharist, it is a real happening
each time, and is more than a date on a calendar.
I believe the angels sing "Alleluia" once more.

The angels may sing in silence or aloud
in our hearts after our long wait.
Our hearts are, after all, where he is born again
and where the real Christmas takes place.

Alleluia. Amen.

Packing Christmas Away

Although there are many who are anxious
to get all the Christmas decorations down and packed away,
there is always a tinge of sadness
of having to take the "jewelry" off.

Perhaps it's facing that Christmas anticipation
is over for another year.
I miss all the roping, the candles, and the tree of memories.
Then I remember my new mantra I read or heard about,
being happy that something happened
instead of being sad that it is over.

What happened was the joy Advent always brings,
even the times that it gets dark.
Watching my children with their children
is indescribable joy.

Contemplating the miracle of Christmas is a lifelong task
that does not end with the epiphany.
Nor does it get packed away in the basement.
(I do have a couple of decorations I keep out all year).

I have no clue how to end this.
Maybe because Christmas has no end
and can never be packed away.
Amen. Alleluia!

The New Year's Phenomena

All around the world, human beings celebrate
the start of a new year.
It is probably one of our greatest characteristics:
HOPE!

No matter the downsides of the previous year
or the reality of the leery changes we know are coming,
the world chooses to celebrate.
It is hope that allows us to do this.

Hope is a sign of an indomitable spirit
we look forward, not backward,
and that keeps us mentally healthy and alive.
We are on the streets in party mode—not hiding in fear.

Hope is a very powerful spirit.
It puts us in the present instead of the past.
I suspect most of the partygoers believe
in some form of God.

Hope is a sign of God's presence,
along with its sister virtue, trust.
No matter how tough the year and circumstances,
we show up to party for the New Year coming.

It takes hope and trust to do that,
qualities that are gifts from God.
Named or unnamed,
there is grace in the midst of the revelry.

CHAPTER XII

Easter

From the Shadow of Golgotha

Although not a place one comes willingly,
obedience now drives my prayer and will,
and so I arrive at the foot of the cross,
albeit trembling.

It looks to be a place filled
with agony, failure, and despair.
The darkness of death falls across the land.

But stepping into the shadow
reminds me of a science lesson
learned long ago—there is only
a shadow because of the light.

During the very throes of death,
Christ hears a confession from one side
and taunting mockery from the other.
Both he receives.
Only one he answers.

My questions start and make their own noise.
Why doesn't it feel crowded with all these people?
How can this place of torture actually be feeling safe?
Why is it I can see in what appears to be so dark?

There are definitely answers here,
But not the ones I thought of or asked.
Paradox again routs all that I know.
In what is a place of chaos,
the clarity of his truth is revealed.

Salvation comes through injustice.
Suffering will end the pain.
Love is the only answer to hate,
and hope will rise out of despair.

It only makes sense if you decide to stay.
He will move you from looking up to out.
You will then see what He sees
and know what He knows.

Those who hate must be loved.
The unjust can be justified,
and those broken by despair
will be raised up.

Sometimes I forget and go off wandering,
back to where sense brings pleasure.
Love is for those who deserve it,
and I dare decide who is good and who is not.

Then I notice that
this place where truth is set by majority,
the "good" are free and the "bad" imprisoned,
does not feel very safe or right.

My crowd of one makes it hard to see,
even to breathe.
It's obvious I have strayed once again.

"Remember where to always stay,"
Fr. Ken emphasized and reiterated.
It seems a strange place to dwell.

But where else would the Father be
if not where his Son loved unto his death
into the heart of His Father?

"I Thirst"

"I thirst"
Two simple words he spoke.
Two words teaching us the way
to carry our crosses,
to die our Calvaries.

This cup we are given to drink,
The Blood of Christ,
As we reach out, "Take this cup and drink,"
do we think of the cup raised at the Last Supper,
or the blood that poured from his wounds
streaming down the hillside of Calvary

Where does our blood pour out
as we follow his way,
serving his people?

Are we giving
with the very substance of our lives?
Our time, energy, love, compassion
our sweat, blood, and tears?

It costs to serve this Lord.
We were instructed on Holy Thursday.
"You must serve…"
Do we resist as quickly and vehemently as Peter?

Is He cruel? Does He want our pain?
"In burnt offerings, I take no delight."

His demands come only from love.
"Love one another as I have loved you."
To be in love, to serve in love, to stay in love.
This is what he asks. This is what he gives.

Can we be a servant as he taught on Thursday?
Do we die in love and obedience as he did on Friday?
As we enter our own hells on Saturday,
do we believe we will rise on Sunday?

Why do we forget what is told in Scriptures
as we wander our own roads to Emmaus?
Maybe we hope or expect it will be different for us
yet it is written.

Blessed are we when we hear again the sacred Word
and hearts again burn within us.
We joyfully return to our mission serving as true believers.

To drink of his cup.

Desire in Her Eyes

Mary of Magdalene alone went searching, weeping
desperate to find the body of her teacher.
The body of her Lord, dead
but still vibrantly alive in the intensity of her love and desire.

She who followed, loved, served, and watched him die
did not recognize him in the garden.
Not until he called her name—"Mary."
How her heart must have leapt as the familiar
voice called her by name.

Were his following words hard for her to hear, to understand?
"Do not cling to me."
How her heart and arms must have ached,
helpless and unable to have protected him from his torture,
to shield him from his persecutors,
to hold and rock his broken body in her arms.

Touch must have been important to her,
or she would not have been there to anoint his body.
Her desire a sacred gift of loving him
love that did not die but resurrected with, and in, his new form.

"Go and tell them."
The desire of love now directed
from her eyes and heart
into the service her loved one called her to do.

Loving him, he called her now to love his people
"Go and tell them.
Go and love them as I have loved you."

Desire now directed.
Love fulfilling love.

Silence into the Passion

Although I cannot describe the quiet,
the reason for it may be noted.
Today I led Lectio at Manresa
The passage was the Agony in the Garden.

When presenting or facilitating,
I don't usually enter in too deeply,
as I am paying attention to the group,
trying to gauge their need.

The group was very good,
and the reading went very deep,
as revealed by their sharing.
It was an honor to be with them.

It has always been difficult for me to meditate on the passion.
The reason I suspect is my hypervigilance to pain.
Yet today I spent time in the Garden with Jesus
while He was in deep conversation with His Father about his fear.

The women in the group focused mostly
on Jesus being overwhelmed
and putting the Father's will above his own.
I was struck that in his agony
He asked his friends to stay by Him.

This puts me in a conundrum.
I use my hypervigilance as an excuse.
Yet there is the awakening to Jesus,
asking his friends to stay with Him.

I have spent many hours at the foot of the cross
but have not been able to spend time with Him
at the scourging and crowning of thorns.
Today He asks me to stay with Him.

How can I say no to such a request?
It's unthinkable now that He has asked.
Am I scared?
Yes, very much so.

The quiet has moved to the noise of the Passion.

Holy Mary

"Holy Mary, who kept the faith on Holy Saturday,
pray for us."

What did you do on Holy Saturday?
Was your prayer based on the promises and prophesies
you had heard over the lifetime of Jesus?
I need to stay with you to learn from your faith.

On this Holy Saturday,
there are threats of war and deportation.

You kept the faith. You knew in your heart it was not over.
It's never over anymore.
Your Son will rise and in doing so conquer death.
We will still die as he did, but we will also rise.

Did you remind the other women and the apostles
of the words you heard Jesus speak?
When He spoke of rebuilding the temple in three days,
I suspect you suspected exactly what he meant.

That is faith.
Mothers know their children yet are
continuously surprised by them.
Were you surprised when you saw Him, or
were you patiently expecting Him?
Of course you grieved over the crucifixion, how could you not?
But I think you knew. Mothers know.

I watched my children and their children play baseball today.
As I watched, there was a thrill of watching
Susie and Jeff play together.
Better yet, they were playing with their kids,
and I was in awe at the skill of the grandkids.

But the lines of you keeping the faith
kept playing through my mind.
Louder even than David J.'s baseball playlist.
And I wondered why.

I thought about the state of our country again
and realized I need to keep the faith
through all this despairing talk of war.
These are my children, and I pray with
faith you will keep them safe.

He Rose in Silence

The greatest miracle of all time
took place in silence.
The earth did not shake,
the skies did not open in storms.

No witnesses.
No crowds.
Jesus rising alone
with no fanfare.

He who was killed in a garbage pit,
among jeering and grieving crowds,
rose alone in sacred silence,
with the Trinity alone present.

This was the humility of the Father.
He performed the greatest miracle
in quiet.
I suspect it was also the greatest act of intimacy.

Jesus started to show Himself,
and his followers were probably
shocked into silence.
They ran to tell the others as instructed.

As word started to spread,
there were no protests at Pilate's palace.
The apostles huddled together in fear,
knowing the Romans would blame them.

People do not rise from the dead,
even if they were told ahead of time.
It would take the Spirit on Pentecost
to free them from their fears.

In the meantime, they spent their time in prayer.
What did this mean?
Why did He do this by Himself?
Did they start to remember His predictions?

He rose in silence and humility.
This was God acting in reverence and intimacy.

Easter Eve

Mary Magdalene was probably not focused on the Sabbath.
Instead, she was probably gathering what she needed
to anoint the body of her loved one.
It was probably the only thing that gave her solace in her grief.

Grief is a powerful and devastating emotion.
Her trauma at the crucifixion
probably blocked her memories of what Jesus had been teaching her.
He had to suffer and die, but He would rise!

That's never happened before so we can't blame her for forgetting.
What was in front of her were the images from yesterday,
of her loved one being tortured and humiliated.
He, who had only taught and behaved in love.

She was probably thrilled when daybreak
came and she could touch his body.
I wanted to touch David's body again. I
wanted to dig up his coffin myself.
Imagine Mary's dismay at seeing the body gone.
I can only imagine her reaction to hearing Him speak her name.

It used to bother me that He told her not to cling to Him.
How could she not follow that primal instinct?
But then He told her he was going to the Father so
The Father could be her Father as well as everyone.

The Father would be her Father?
The Father that Jesus was so totally in love with,
that he died for us?
The Father that he would go off by himself to converse with?

Jesus was going to His Father to make him "our Father."
Having traveled with Jesus, she knew how close they were.
And now He was going to be our Father.
Was it like a bolt of lightning when she realized who
Jesus was that he could say "My Father"?

I can only imagine the speed at which she ran
when Jesus sent her to tell the others.
She was so filled with joy she did not even care
they had to go check for themselves.

He called her name: "Mary."
Something she would never forget,
and would ponder the rest of her days.

Easter Sunday Night

Only upon seeing His figure against the moonlight
do I come out of hiding to meet him.
He knows I would have heard the stories…
He has risen!

Hoping against all hope, I prayed
he would come to our meeting place.
As he comes closer
I go running, laughing, and crying.

I touch his scars
as new understanding and belief
flood my entire being,
replacing grief and despair.

"Look at me" is all he says,
lifting my chin to face him.
With love and desire, I search his eyes,
and I see God.

Easter Monday Consolation

It feels like...
As I keep pondering on what Jesus's loved ones
must have felt on Easter Monday,
I am filled with the same exuberant yet mysterious consolation.

Our faith has many mysteries, and resurrection is one.
People do not rise from the dead.
Jesus is God so that is not the mystery.
The mystery is He is also human.

How do we wrap our minds around that?
No one was there when he rose;
that does not matter to all the people to whom he appeared.
They knew he died, and now he was alive.

And why am I being given the same consolation,
the same questions, the same awe?
He is present with me so the miracle
of two thousand years past still takes place today.

"Jesus died, Jesus rose, Jesus will come again."
He will come again in physical form,
but the spiritual form is real to me today.
He has come again. And again...

St. Ignatius named it consolation.
Many may doubt it.
Unless you have experienced this presence,
then you just know it.

It is a presence that is mysterious
yet it is also beyond doubt.
There is a certainty that it is "I am."
He comes bearing the Good News.

Still Human and Divine

The scars were not erased through the resurrection.
Jesus was still human and divine.
Something that is difficult to grasp,
except that He showed us what it meant.

He looked different, yet his essence remained,
and so people were able to recognize Him.
Mary recognized his voice.
John and Peter recognized Him on the shore.

As human and divine,
did He rise thinking "I knew it!"
Or was it memory fully divinized, and
He remembered, volunteering to come and save us?

In the spiritual exercises,
Ignatius has us visit his appearance to his mother.
It is written that he said "Mary" to the Magdalene.
I can only imagine the name was spoken with great tenderness.

He cooked for his disciples on the seashore.
He knew where to find them.
He knew how to feed them.
They all were hungry and Jesus served them.

He wore his scars in silence,
the only exception was Thomas who needed proof.
A mother does not tell her child of the painful birth
because love overcomes the pain.

Jesus, immersed in divine love, does not need
to talk of the pain of his Passion
because love overcomes the pain.

He just wanted to be with his disciples,
betrayal or no betrayal.
He taught us to forgive...
"Peter, do you love me?"

He asks of us the same question, and we have the same answer.
"You know we love you, Lord."
We are taught how to forgive.
Our divinization begins.

ACKNOWLEDGMENTS

The first people I need to thank are my children—David, Jeff, and Susie—for accepting their mother as she is. We went through some very exciting, and also dark times together. Those times are real and does not matter if they are spoken or are unspoken. Thank you for your acceptance. There aren't enough words to convey how much respect and awe I have of you, and what amazing people and parents you are. Thank you. To my magnificent seven, grandchildren, who teach me about God every day: David, Anthony, Dan, Lucy, Charlie, Jane and Joey. To the perfect spouses, my son in law, Dan and daughter in law, Debbie. I love you all.

To my brother, Jerry, a retired Houston police officer, for his wisdom, common sense, listening, and love. To his adorable wife, Sue; son Bryan, and his soon-to-be-wife, Katy. To the German extension of family. We miss you.

Thank you to the entire past and present staff of Manresa Jesuit Retreat House in Michigan, for your ongoing formation and support, from your care on my yearly retreats to comings and goings for spiritual directing. Thank you to the peer supervision group who meet monthly. You are each real gift.

My friends Debbie Rivers, Lesley Palmeri, Bob Connor, Judy Gumbel, Fr. Bernie, Anne Smith, and Pat Seibold as well as my renewed friendship with fellow sorority sisters from the University of Detroit. I also want to thank all the people who have trusted me to have been students, clients and spiritual directees, for I have learned more from you than I have given.

ABOUT THE AUTHOR

Denise Anderson is a spiritual director and counselor from Rochester Hills, Michigan. She lives near her children and grandchildren, whom she loves spending time with. Her formation as a spiritual director took place at Manresa Jesuit Retreat House. She was a teacher and counselor in the East Detroit and Chippewa Valley School Systems and at St. Anne Catholic School in Warren. For fifteen years, she studied the Christian Spiritual Classics with Reverend Bernie Owens, SJ, author of <u>More Than You Can Ever Imagine</u> On Our Becoming Divine (Liturgical Press). Denise presents journal prayer workshops and talks on spirituality as well as guides people through the spiritual exercises of St. Ignatius.

CPSIA information can be obtained
at www.ICGtesting.com
Printed in the USA
FFHW021845021218
49686066-54077FF